STUDY GUIDE SIX SESSIONS

relat(able)

MAKING RELATIONSHIPS WORK

LOUIE GIGLIO

WITH DIXON KINSER

THOMAS NELSON
Since 1798

passionpublishing

Relat(able) Study Guide

Published in Nashville, Tennessee, by Thomas Nelson. Thomas Nelson is a registered trademark of HarperCollins Christian Publishing, Inc.

ISBN 978-0-310-08872-1

May 2016 / Printed in the United States of America

CONTENTS

INTRODUCTION

One of the great mysteries of the Christian faith is the Holy Trinity. The doctrine of the Trinity developed over centuries and reflects the church's consistent witness that, though God is one God, he exists as three persons. Those persons are called Father, Son, and Holy Spirit, and each is distinct: the Father is not the Son, the Son is not the Spirit, and the Spirit is not the Father. Yet while each of the persons of the Trinity remains distinct, God continues to be one.

If that makes your head spin a little, it's okay. That is why the Trinity is considered a holy mystery. God is always bigger than our minds can fully comprehend. Yet at the heart of the Trinity is a profound truth that has endured for millennia: *God's very being is relationship*. The flow of love from Son to Spirit, and Spirit to Father, and Father to Son is the essence of who God is. This is good news for people like us, because all of us want better relationships. We long for connections that are meaningful, fulfilling, and significant. Whether it is a desire to be a healthier parent, spouse, partner, or friend, or to have greater capacity to forgive and reconcile with those who have hurt us, we do not need to worry. God has everything we need, because no one is better at relationships than God. It is, literally, what God is all about. Helping you tap into that power and be transformed is what this study is all about too.

The title of the series is *Relat(able)* because during this study you are going to explore a simple but weighty question: "How do you relate?" Each session will discuss a different facet of this question by engaging the stories of the Bible and the teaching of Louie Giglio. In each gathering, expect an opening question, a short Bible study, and then some time with Louie via video. However, the real action comes when you dig in to each topic during a guided small group experience. During this time your group will be invited to participate in a practical activity designed to move the session's *Relat(able)* lesson from your head to your heart. This section is called "Becoming Relat(able)," and it will serve as a place where the big ideas of this study take on some flesh-and-blood reality.

In addition, there are two bonus sessions included in this study: "Why Date?" and "Marriage with a Mission." If your group is primarily comprised of singles who are dating (or are considering dating), you may elect to have the participants study the material in the first bonus session: "Why Date?" If your group is primarily comprised of married couples, you may find it beneficial for the participants to study the material in the second bonus session: "Marriage with a Mission." The discussion guide for these sessions can be found at the end of this book.

It's going to be great! However, if you want to get the most out of your *Relat(able)* experience, you need to keep a couple of things in mind. First, the real growth in this study will happen during your small group time. This is where you will process the content of Louie's message, ask questions, and learn from others as you listen to what God is doing in their lives.

This leads to point two: As much as small groups can be a deeply rewarding time of intimacy and friendship, they can also be a disaster. Work to make your group a "safe place." That means both being honest about your thoughts and feelings as well as listening carefully to everyone else's opinion.

Third, resist the temptation to "fix" a problem someone might be experiencing, or to correct his or her theology. That's not what this time is for. Finally, keep everything your group shares confidential. All this will foster a rewarding sense of community in your *Relat(able)* group and give God space to do something new in the relationships in your life.

HOW TO USE THIS GUIDE

Relat(able) is designed to be as personal as is it practical. Each session begins with a mixer question followed by a reflection from the Bible. Then you'll watch the video with Louie and jump into some directed small group discussion. Even though there are many questions available for your small group, don't feel like you have to use them all. Your leader will focus on the ones that resonate most with your group and guide you from there.

The final component of each session is called "Becoming Relat(able)." This is where *Relat(able)* might diverge from other studies you have experienced. In this part of the study, your group will engage in a hands-on practical exercise that seeks to move the good news of the session from your head to your heart. Think of this time as an answer to the question, "What am I supposed to *do* with this message?"

These exercises are meant to be completed during your meeting time, and they will be what you make of them. If you choose to only go through the motions, or if you abstain from participating, there is a lesser chance you'll find what you're looking for in this study. But if you stay open-minded and take a chance, you may discover what so many others have already found to be true: faith comes alive when we take holy risks for God.

Now, it is understandable that the thought of "risky" activities makes you feel anxious. That's okay. If you fall into this category, just read ahead to each "Becoming Relat(able)" section and you will know not only what's coming up but also how to prepare yourself accordingly. Finally, remember that none of these exercises involves anything inappropriate or embarrassing. They are just hands-on opportunities to keep us open to God's love and to help us see the gospel as true good news.

Following your group time, there will be three more opportunities for you to engage the content of *Relat(able)* during the week. Each is based on one of the three central relationships of love that Louie speaks to in the study. The first one focuses on our relationship with God (*Love God*), the second addresses the way we love ourselves (*Love Yourself*), and the third is about how we can better love our neighbors (*Love Your Neighbor*). The challenge will be to do at least one of these activities between sessions and to use this study guide to record what you learn.

Starting in Session 2, you will have time before the video to check in about the previous week's activity and process your experiences as a group. And, if you could not do an activity one week, or are just joining the study, don't worry. Hearing what others have learned will be nourishment enough.

Finally, remember that all this is an opportunity to train in a new way of relating. The videos, discussions, and activities are simply meant to kick-start your imagination so you are not only open to God's love but also start letting it change you from the inside out. Consider what God could do with a whole group of people who were open to receiving his love, grace, and mercy, and then wanted to see that same love, grace, and mercy transform all their relationships. How would that change their lives? How would it change their community? How would it change their city? Let's jump into *Relat(able)* and find out.

IF YOU ARE A GROUP LEADER there are additional instructions and resources in the back of this book. Because some of the activities require materials and setup, make sure you read this over so you will be prepared.

---

session (I)

THE SHOVEL AND THE SPOON

Are you the kind of person who's going to move through life being able to have relationships that are meaningful and fulfilling and significant? Are you able to relate?

Louie Giglio

Orientation

If you have ever been near schoolchildren on a playground, one of the things you are bound to overhear is the accusation, "That's not fair!" Indeed, fairness and a sense of equality is something children carry with them from a very early age. This has much to do, of course, with the deep need for justice God has placed in all of us. It also has something to do with what we learned, early on, to expect from life: that at its best, everything should come out "even" in the end.

But here's the problem. As Christians, we know from the crucifixion of Jesus that life, justice, and even God are not fair. Life is not fair because of the sin that corrupts and destroys the people of God. Justice is not fair because God's justice is accomplished by an act of supreme unfairness, Jesus' death on the cross. And God himself is not fair because in spite of what people may deserve, God keeps offering grace to everyone. This is who God is. God can't help it. God is a mercy giver, and in a world that thirsts for fairness, sometimes this can be hard to accept.

This week in *Relat(able)*, Louie kicks off the series by drawing connections between our love of God, our neighbors, and ourselves. He argues that if one of these loving relationships gets out of order, it will skew the other two as well. They are all connected in a kind of dynamic interdependence, and what fuels them is God's radical mercy and love for his people.

Louie also suggests that our relational health might have as much to do with our ability to receive mercy as it does with our ability to give it, which brings us back to fairness. The kind of mercy God offers is not fair. It just is not. We did not earn it. We cannot justify it, and yet it is there, available to us, every day. This week's session is about opening up to this kind of radical, unfair love. The kind of love that is at the heart of what God is doing in Christ. The kind of love that is changing the world. The kind of love that can also change lives.

When we open up to this kind of love, everything changes. The question for this week is, "Are you open to that?"

Welcome and Checking In

Go around the group and invite the members to introduce themselves, and then answer the following questions:

> Which scenario recharges your batteries: spending time with people, or spending time alone?
>
> If you could describe your hopes for this study in one word, that word would be: ___________. Why did you answer the way you did?

Hearing the Word

Read Matthew 20:1 – 16 aloud in the group. Invite everyone to listen for a fresh insight during the reading.

> [1] *For the kingdom of heaven is like a landowner who went out early in the morning to hire workers for his vineyard.* [2] *He agreed to pay them a denarius for the day and sent them into his vineyard.*

3 About nine in the morning he went out and saw others standing in the marketplace doing nothing. 4 He told them, "You also go and work in my vineyard, and I will pay you whatever is right." 5 So they went.

He went out again about noon and about three in the afternoon and did the same thing. 6 About five in the afternoon he went out and found still others standing around. He asked them, "Why have you been standing here all day long doing nothing?"

7 "Because no one has hired us," they answered.

He said to them, "You also go and work in my vineyard."

8 When evening came, the owner of the vineyard said to his foreman, "Call the workers and pay them their wages, beginning with the last ones hired and going on to the first."

9 The workers who were hired about five in the afternoon came and each received a denarius. 10 So when those came who were hired first, they expected to receive more. But each one of them also received a denarius. 11 When they received it, they began to grumble against the landowner. 12 "These who were hired last worked only one hour," they said, "and you have made them equal to us who have borne the burden of the work and the heat of the day."

13 But he answered one of them, "I am not being unfair to you, friend. Didn't you agree to work for a denarius? 14 Take your pay and go. I want to give the one who was hired last the same as I gave you. 15 Don't I have the right to do what I want with my own money? Or are you envious because I am generous?"

16 So the last will be first, and the first will be last.

In groups of two or three, share your answers to the following questions:

What was one thing that stood out to you from the reading? Was this a new insight?

What situation do you imagine Jesus might have been addressing when he told this parable?

What does this parable have to say about "fairness"? Does God have a different definition than we do?

Watch the Video

Play the video segment for Session 1. As you watch, use the following outline to record any thoughts or concepts that stand out to you.

Notes

The degree to which we receive what God has given to us determines the degree to which we are able to have meaningful relationships with ourselves and with other people.

Two reasons why we don't accept what God wants to give us: (1) we don't think we're worthy, and (2) we don't believe that what he has to offer is better than what we currently have.

Apart from our relationship with God, our relationship with ourselves is the most important relationship we will have in this life.

The number one flaw we experience in relationships is that we expect more of other people than they can realistically give and be in our lives.

Jesus can relate to us because (1) he took on the constraints of entering into time and space, and (2) he took on flesh and blood and became human just like us.

Jesus relates to us by (1) not giving us what we deserve, and (2) coming all the way to find us and show us mercy. This affects how we relate, because in the same measure we receive this love, we are able to extend that love to others.

Group Discussion

Take a few minutes with your group members to discuss what you just watched and explore these concepts in Scripture.

First Impressions

1. Before everyone shares in the large group, turn to one or two people next to you and finish this sentence: "After watching the video, one question I now have is ..."

Community Reflection

2. Do you consider yourself a people person? Why did you answer the way you did?

3. What is one thing you learned about relationships from the family you grew up in?

4. In the video, Louie notes that a primary flaw we experience in relationships is that we expect more of other people than they can realistically provide. Do you think this is true? Why or why not?

5. We are *beloved*; it is our identity in Christ. Which is harder for you to do: to be honestly critical of yourself or to receive praise? Why did you answer the way you did?

6. Louie remarks that what we expect from others is certainly not what we want all the time from God. We want him to give us way more grace than we give to other people. Do you relate to this statement? If so, how? If not, why not?

7. In the Matthew 20 parable, Jesus challenges his audience to consider the ways they resent God's lavish grace being shown to people they think are undeserving. Have you ever felt as if there was someone who did not deserve God's grace? Has that person ever been you? Did you learn anything from Louie in this session that helped?

Becoming Relat(able)

For this activity, each participant will need a blank piece of paper, a pen, and an envelope.

In this session, you have explored what it means to be able to relate. It involves health in three relationships: your relationship with God, your relationship with yourself, and your relationship with others.

Take a few minutes to pray, and then answer the following question on one side of the piece of paper you have been given: *If God could grow me in one of these relationships, which one would it be, and how would I want to grow?* Be as honest as you can be. No one will ever see it but you.

Once you have written your answer, write any specifics you want to include about the relationship and then seal it in your envelope. Finally, as a sign of being open to God's movement in this area of your life and accepting God's view of you, write the word *beloved* on the outside of the envelope.

Put the envelope in the pages of this study guide. Each week when you return to your guide, let it be a reminder to you of your prayer and how God sees you. You are *beloved.*

Closing Prayer

Close the session by reading Psalm 103 aloud as a prayer:

> 1 *Praise the Lord, my soul;*
> *all my inmost being, praise his holy name.*
> 2 *Praise the Lord, my soul,*
> *and forget not all his benefits—*
> 3 *who forgives all your sins*
> *and heals all your diseases,*
> 4 *who redeems your life from the pit*
> *and crowns you with love and compassion,*
> 5 *who satisfies your desires with good things*
> *so that your youth is renewed like the eagle's.*
> 6 *The Lord works righteousness*
> *and justice for all the oppressed.*
> 7 *He made known his ways to Moses,*
> *his deeds to the people of Israel:*
> 8 *The Lord is compassionate and gracious,*
> *slow to anger, abounding in love.*
> 9 *He will not always accuse,*
> *nor will he harbor his anger forever;*
> 10 *he does not treat us as our sins deserve*
> *or repay us according to our iniquities.*
> 11 *For as high as the heavens are above the earth,*
> *so great is his love for those who fear him;*

12 as far as the east is from the west,
so far has he removed our transgressions from us.
13 As a father has compassion on his children,
so the LORD has compassion on those who fear him;
14 for he knows how we are formed,
he remembers that we are dust.
15 The life of mortals is like grass,
they flourish like a flower of the field;
16 the wind blows over it and it is gone,
and its place remembers it no more.
17 But from everlasting to everlasting
the LORD's love is with those who fear him,
and his righteousness with their children's children—
18 with those who keep his covenant
and remember to obey his precepts.
19 The LORD has established his throne in heaven,
and his kingdom rules over all.
20 Praise the LORD, you his angels,
you mighty ones who do his bidding,
who obey his word.
21 Praise the LORD, all his heavenly hosts,
you his servants who do his will.
22 Praise the LORD, all his works
everywhere in his dominion.
Praise the LORD, my soul. Amen.

(**Note:** You can also read this psalm responsively by whole verse. The leader would read verse 1, and the group would read verse 2 in response, and so on.)

BETWEEN-SESSIONS PERSONAL STUDY

You are invited to further explore the good news of *Relat(able)* by engaging in any or all of the following between-sessions activities. Remember, this part of the *Relat(able)* experience is not about following rules or doing your homework. Rather these activities—arranged according to their purpose of growing your relationship with *God*, *self*, and *neighbor*—are designed to give you an opportunity to be open to God and his work in your relationships. *Be sure to read the reflection questions after each activity and make a few notes in your guide about the experience.* There will be a time to share these reflections at the beginning of the next session.

Love God: Get a Mercy Shovel

The name of this session is "The Shovel and the Spoon," based on Louie's metaphor that when it comes to mercy, God heaps it on with a huge shovel, not a spoon. In the last part of this week's video, Louie says, "When you wake up tomorrow, just imagine that there is an angel standing by your bed, and he's just shoveling mercy and pouring it on you before you even hit the snooze button." In this activity, you are invited to do more than just imagine—you are invited to make this a reality each day this week.

First, get an actual shovel. This can be a big shovel, a small shovel, a new shovel, or one lying around your garage.

Second, write the word *mercy* on the blade of the shovel. You can use a sticky note, a paint pen, or a felt-tipped marker. Whatever you choose, just make sure the word *mercy* is unmissable in the way it is attached to the shovel.

Third, take your "mercy shovel" into your bedroom and prop it up beside your bed or someplace else obvious. You can even arrange it so that it will get in your way. Wherever you put it, make sure you will see it every day this week.

Once you have set up your mercy shovel, use it as a devotional tool. Each time you see it, let it act as a reminder of the mercy, grace, and love that God has for you. God's mercy is new every morning, so let this be a daily reminder to you of that fact. Respond with a prayer of thanksgiving, or just take a deep breath as a way of receiving God's unconditional grace and love.

It's for you.

No strings attached.

No matter what.

By the shovel-full.

(**Note:** You can also do this activity by carrying a small garden spade with you this week. Take this small shovel with you to the office, or to school, or in the car. This would be another way to practice constant awareness of God's radical, overwhelming, ever-new mercy.)

Take note of how God uses this activity to speak to you. Make a few notes about it below to share with the group next week.

Pray. God is near.

The love of God trumps whatever else we have experienced in life. The fundamental idea is not what our dad was like and not what our mom was like, because we can't change that. The fundamental idea is how willing we are and what is our capacity to receive what God is wanting to give us today. That is going to be the number one shaper of our ability to have a meaningful and successful relationship with ourselves and with the people around us.

Louie Giglio, Relat(able) *video*

Love Yourself: Have Fun!

In the video this week, Louie says that our ability to have healthy interpersonal relationships is directly connected with our ability to love God and love ourselves. Louie's connections are built on the words of Jesus, who said that the second greatest commandment in all of the Law is to love your neighbor as yourself (see Matthew 22:36 – 40). So, it stands to reason that if the way you love yourself gets off track, it might skew your other relationships as well.

For most of us, loving ourselves in a healthy way is an underdeveloped skill and spiritual practice. We train in loving God through worship and prayer, and we train in loving our neighbors through service and fellowship. However, when it comes to loving ourselves, we do not have many practices on which to draw. That is, until now …

This week you are invited to practice loving yourself in a holy, righteous, and Christ-centered way—by doing something fun, just for *you*! This could be seeing a movie, taking time to read, going on a bike ride, or visiting a museum. Whatever it is, make sure it's something that gives you life and restores you.

Remember to pay attention to anything God shows you during this time, and make a few notes about your experience to share with the group next week.

Now, get out there and do something fun for you.

This week.

In the name of Jesus.

God's mercies are new every single day. So when you wake up tomorrow, just imagine there is an angel standing by the bed, and he's just shoveling mercy. He's pouring it on you before you even hit the snooze button. This is not yesterday's mercy. This is new mercy today. We've got lots of angels, and lots of shovels, and it's like "mercy on your life today . . . mercy on your life . . . big shovel of mercy on your life."

Louie Giglio, Relat(able)

Love Your Neighbor: Alone Together

In 2012, Sherry Turkle (professor in the Program in Science, Technology, and Society at MIT and the founder and director of the MIT Initiative on Technology and Self) gave a TED talk where she observed that technology is not just changing *what we do* but also changing *who we are*. One of the primary ways we are being changed is in our ability to relate to one another.

For this exercise, watch Turkle's TED talk at the TED website (http://www.ted.com/talks/sherry_turkle_alone_together), and reflect on the following questions:

- Do you think our communication technology is a good thing or a bad thing? Why did you answer the way you did?
- Turkle makes an important distinction between *connection* and *conversation*. Do you agree with her observation?
- At the end of her talk, Turkle advocates for cultivating the practice of solitude. She argues that learning how

to be alone is what will help us know how to relate to others in the rest of our life. Do you think she's right? Is being alone hard or easy for you? Why?

- Three of the Gospels tell us the first thing Jesus did after his baptism was go into the wilderness where he fasted for forty days. Read one of the accounts of this event in Matthew 4:1 – 11, Mark 1:12 – 13, or Luke 4:1 – 13. Was it easy for Jesus when he was alone? What is the connection between faithful solitude and trusting God with the hardest things we are called to do?
- How does Sherry Turkle's talk relate to Louie's message from *Relat(able)* this week?

Use the space below to write any key points or questions you want to bring to the next group meeting.

session (2)

THE MAN/WOMAN IN THE MIRROR

Our most important relationship is our relationship with ourselves, and our relationship with ourselves is informed by God's love for us.

Louie Giglio

Orientation

Did you ever ride a seesaw as a child? Maybe you knew it by a different name — a teeter-totter or a teeterboard — but whatever you called it, the experience was the same. One person sits on one end, while another sits on the other. As one goes up, the other goes down, and vice versa.

The seesaw, with its simple but delightful lever-and-fulcrum design, has delighted young and old alike for more than a century and has remained a playground staple for generations. That is, of course, unless you have ridden the seesaw with someone who was not your same size. Then the delight of the seesaw can quickly turn into frustration. When there is a mismatch on either end of the seesaw, the device just does not work. It gets out of balance, off kilter, and can even be dangerous.

One time, Jesus was asked by a religious expert which of the 613 commandments in the Hebrew law was the most important. It was a bit of a trick question, but Jesus' answer was brilliant: *Love God with everything you've got, and love your neighbor as yourself.* These two commandments, he said, sum up every one of the 613, because nothing trumps them (see Mark 12:28 – 31).

Jesus knew there was a powerful dynamic between the way we love God, the way we love our neighbor, and the way we love ourselves. They all go together, like the two ends of a seesaw. If one gets out of whack, overemphasized, or neglected, it can throw the other two off balance — and vice versa. It is, therefore, critical that we learn to properly love ourselves, because without that piece, our seesaw will not work.

In this week's session, Louie invites you to consider how you are doing at loving the person you see in the mirror. Is it easy or hard for you to love yourself? Do you ever fall into self-criticism? Have you ever worried that you were not worth loving? These are real questions, and sometimes they emerge from dark and painful places. If that's you, it's okay. Although we will explore some of these questions during this session, you only need to be where you are right now. The intent this week is not to rip the Band-Aid off any old wounds or dredge up painful hurts. You're also not going to be asked to disclose anything you don't want to disclose.

That being said, however, please do take this session head-on and be as honest, open, and real as you can be. What God has in mind for you is too amazing, and he wants to give you tools in this session to love yourself the way he does!

Welcome and Checking In

Go around the group and invite everyone to answer one of the following questions:

> If you were to get a tattoo, what would it say or what would the graphic be?
>
> If you already have a tattoo, what are the words or graphic, and why did you get it?

Last week you were invited to participate in the "Between Sessions" section of the study.

- Did you do one of the activities? If so, which one? If not, why not?

- What are some of the things you wrote down in reflection?
- What did you learn by engaging in these activities?

Hearing the Word

Read Luke 10:25–37 aloud in the group. Invite everyone to listen for a fresh insight during the reading.

25 On one occasion an expert in the law stood up to test Jesus.
"Teacher," he asked, "what must I do to inherit eternal life?"
26 "What is written in the Law?" he replied. "How do you
read it?"
27 He answered, " 'Love the Lord your God with all your
heart and with all your soul and with all your strength and
with all your mind'; and, 'Love your neighbor as yourself.' "
28 "You have answered correctly," Jesus replied. "Do this
and you will live."
29 But he wanted to justify himself, so he asked Jesus, "And
who is my neighbor?"
30 In reply Jesus said: "A man was going down from
Jerusalem to Jericho, when he was attacked by robbers. They
stripped him of his clothes, beat him and went away, leaving
him half dead. 31 A priest happened to be going down the same
road, and when he saw the man, he passed by on the other
side. 32 So too, a Levite, when he came to the place and saw
him, passed by on the other side. 33 But a Samaritan, as he
traveled, came where the man was; and when he saw him,
he took pity on him. 34 He went to him and bandaged his
wounds, pouring on oil and wine. Then he put the man on

his own donkey, brought him to an inn and took care of him.
35 The next day he took out two denarii and gave them to the
innkeeper. 'Look after him,' he said, 'and when I return, I
will reimburse you for any extra expense you may have.'
36 "Which of these three do you think was a neighbor to
the man who fell into the hands of robbers?"
37 The expert in the law replied, "The one who had mercy
on him."
Jesus told him, "Go and do likewise."

Turn to the person next to you and take turns sharing your answers to the following questions:

What was one thing that stood out to you from the reading? Was this a new insight for you?

Jesus tells this parable in reply to a question. What question was he answering?

If the Samaritans were the mortal and sworn enemies of the Jewish people in Jesus' day, what is the point of this parable?

Watch the Video

Play the video segment for Session 2. As you watch, use the following outline to record any thoughts or concepts that stand out to you.

Notes

We are most influenced by ourselves. We hear the voice of ourselves more than any other voice, and are influenced by our thoughts more than anything else. Given this, if we don't have a good relationship with ourselves, we won't have good relationships with others.

God wants us to embrace his love for us and translate that into love for ourselves, because he knows that in the same way we love ourselves we will love our neighbors.

God wants us to get to the place where when we look into the mirror, we actually see what God sees in us and hear what God says about us.

When God looks at us in the "mirror," he says: (1) I love you, (2) I'm thankful for you, (3) you are a rare and beautiful treasure, (4) I forgive you, (5) you are here for a special purpose, (6) I am going to hold you to a high standard, and (7) I believe in you.

If we spent our time cheering ourselves on in the power of the Spirit rather than beating ourselves up, our lives would look so different. We would be champions for Jesus.

God the Father—our perfect Father—the Son, and the Holy Spirit believe in us and are cheering us on with a great company of the heavenly host. When that truth gets into our hearts, we can look in the mirror and say, *I have vision for what God is going to do in my life today.*

Group Discussion

Take a few minutes with your group members to discuss what you just watched and explore these concepts in Scripture.

First Impressions

1. Before everyone shares in the large group, turn to one or two people next to you and finish this sentence: "After watching the video, one question I now have is . . ."

Community Reflection

2. In the video, Louie notes that you are someone who is being cheered for today. Is this hard or easy for you to believe? Do you experience God as someone who cheers for you? Why or why not?

3. What is the difference between *humility* and *self-loathing*?

4. How can we as Christians humble ourselves and not think too highly of ourselves, yet also cheer for ourselves?

5. Louie notes in the video that it does not honor Jesus for us to be really hard on ourselves. Can you relate to this statement? Do you ever beat yourself up? What triggers that kind of behavior?

6. What is the connection between this week's message and the parable of the Good Samaritan?

7. On a scale of 1 to 10, with 1 being easy and 10 being hard, how difficult is it for you to be gracious with yourself when you make a mistake? Why did you answer the way you did?

Becoming Relat(able)

For this activity, each participant will need either a newspaper, magazine, or smartphone.

In the parable Jesus tells about the Good Samaritan, his point is that we are to love the people who are the most disgusting, difficult, and distasteful to us. In short, we are to love our enemies and the people we hate.

Take one of the newspapers, magazines, or smartphones and look through some current domestic or international events. Who is the person, or the people, who are hardest for you to think about loving? Use the space below to jot down who it is and list some of the reasons why it is hard for you to love them. Feel free to be as specific or general as you want here.

Next, think of someone or a group of people in your personal life who are the most difficult to love. This would be someone you have personal contact with but struggle to love. You may even consider them an enemy. Jot down any specifics in the space below, just like before.

We can learn to love our neighbor—even seemingly "unlovable" ones—by better loving ourselves. So, consider two ways you could love *yourself* more this week that would also help you to better love these unlovable people in your life. If they drive you crazy and you need patience, consider having more patience with yourself. If you feel as if you can't forgive them, ask where you can be more forgiving of yourself. Take a few moments to reflect on this and write down anything you discover.

Closing Prayer

Invite the group to share anything they wrote down, and then close the session by going around the circle and having everyone offer a one-word prayer for the ways they want to better love themselves this week.

BETWEEN-SESSIONS PERSONAL STUDY

Further explore the good news of *Relat(able)* this week by engaging in any or all of the following between-sessions activities. *Be sure to read the reflection questions after each activity and make a few notes in your guide about the experience.* There will be a time to share these reflections at the beginning of the next session.

Love God: Listen Up

In the video this week, we examined how listening to God's words about us can be transformative. When we attach ourselves to the living words of God, start listening to what he says about us, and start seeing what he sees in us, we can then start speaking what God speaks over us. In this activity, we are going to road test this teaching.

First, consider the seven phrases we examined that God says to us in the mirror:

1. I love you.
2. I'm thankful for you.
3. You are a rare and beautiful treasure.
4. I forgive you.
5. You are here for a special purpose.
6. I am holding you to a high standard.
7. I believe in you.

Which one is easiest for you to hear? Which one is the most difficult? Why?

Next, grab a piece of paper and some tape, or a sticky note, and write the phrase or phrases that are the *most difficult* for you to hear. Put this on the mirror you look at most often. Read the phrase every time you see it, and let it be a reminder of what God says about you when he sees you in the mirror. Let God use it to challenge you and love you into a better future.

Why would we beat ourselves up when Jesus was beaten up for us? The beating, friends, is finished. We have been forgiven. Yes, the Scripture says we should buffet the body, but it never says buffet the soul. Buffeting the body is just to ensure we make it to the finish line in life. The soul needs to be nurtured in an incubator of the truth of what God says about who we are, and the love and the grace that he's poured out for us in the person of Jesus Christ.

Louie Giglio, Relat(able)

Love Yourself: "With You I Am Well Pleased"

Begin by reading the following passage from Exodus 1:8 – 14:

> *8 Then a new king, to whom Joseph meant nothing, came to power in Egypt. 9 "Look," he said to his people, "the Israelites have become far too numerous for us. 10 Come, we must deal shrewdly with them or they will become even more numerous and, if war breaks out, will join our enemies, fight against us and leave the country."*
>
> *11 So they put slave masters over them to oppress them with forced labor, and they built Pithom and Rameses as store cities for Pharaoh. 12 But the more they were oppressed, the more they multiplied and spread; so the Egyptians came to dread the Israelites 13 and worked them ruthlessly. 14 They made their lives bitter with harsh labor in brick and mortar and with all kinds of work in the fields; in all their harsh labor the Egyptians worked them ruthlessly.*

Bricks.

All day.

Every day.

For the Israelites in Egypt, this was their life. They were slaves, and their worth was determined by what they could produce. This is the way slavery works. *Produce for your master, or else.* So this was the life in Egypt ... making bricks for Pharaoh. All day. Every day. And if for any reason you could not make bricks, then you were no longer valuable and could be discarded.

This kind of existence is one of the paradigmatic pictures of the Bible's definition of slavery, and it is what motivates God to free Israel. As slaves, God's people are not only miserable but also not deemed fully human. God made humans for so much more, yet the slavery dynamic distorts God's best by giving the people a skewed sense of worth. Being valuable for only what you produce is not an existence that is fitting for God's people.

Things aren't that much different for us today. Too often we derive our worth from what we make or do. Whether it's at work, home, or even our hobbies, we as humans have a propensity to end up drifting toward the rhythms of Egypt, searching for significance in our ability to produce. Remember that the word for this in the Bible is *slavery*, because that's what it is.

Take, as a contrast, God's words spoken over Jesus at his baptism. The story is told in Matthew 3:13–17:

> [13] *Then Jesus came from Galilee to the Jordan to be baptized*
> *by John.* [14] *But John tried to deter him, saying, "I need to be baptized by you, and do you come to me?"*
>
> [15] *Jesus replied, "Let it be so now; it is proper for us to do this to fulfill all righteousness." Then John consented.*
>
> [16] *As soon as Jesus was baptized, he went up out of the water. At that moment heaven was opened, and he saw the Spirit of God descending like a dove and alighting on him.*
> [17] *And a voice from heaven said, "This is my Son, whom I love; with him I am well pleased."*

The voice of God proclaims to the world, "This is my Son, whom I love; with him I am well pleased." One of the things so radical about this proclamation is that it happens at the beginning of Jesus' ministry. No healings thus far. No miracles. No prayers. No sermons. No parables. Nothing aside from just being a person who trusts God with everything he's got.

In other words, Jesus has value to God, and he hasn't produced anything yet. This is important because even though Jesus was fully God at his baptism, God's pleasure was not in response to that quality. No, God's pleasure, love, and acceptance came *in spite of* what Jesus could or would do. Jesus did not earn God's favor and love—it just came to him as a gift, not a reward. And that is how it comes to us as well.

There is no more slavery for us in Christ Jesus. God does not value us based on what we do. The question, then, is do you believe that?

- Do you ever feel as if you get your worth from what you do? If so, where has that led you?
- How can you keep your God-given capacity to make, create, and work with God from drifting into the slavery of "brick making"?
- What part of your life feels as if it drifts into "brick making" the most?
- Do you believe that God could say that he is pleased with you? Why or why not?

Make a few notes about your experience to share with the group next week.

> *The gospel hangs in the balance of you believing what God has said is true about you. The people in the world are only going to get the love with which you love yourself. That's what they're going to get. When they start living with you and hanging out with you, what they're going to get about Jesus is whatever you have received about him. I don't know what noise, what curse, what lie got you out of sync, but I know the voice of the Shepherd who can sing you back into the melody.*
>
> *Louie Giglio,* Relat(able)

Love Your Neighbor: To Write Love on Her Arms

The organization To Write Love on Her Arms (TWLOHA) is a great example of the way God is healing past pain and teaching people to love themselves as he does. TWLOHA is a nonprofit movement dedicated to presenting hope and finding help for people struggling with depression, addiction, self-injury, and suicide. TWLOHA inspires individuals and invests directly in treatment and recovery. It is a pretty amazing organization doing real life-saving work.

For this exercise, link over to the TWLOHA website (https://twloha.com/learn/) and read the information about this ministry and its mission. When you are finished, answer the following:

- How does telling people that they are not alone in their pain help to heal them?
- TWLOHA says, "We often ask God to show up. We pray prayers of rescue. Perhaps God would ask *us* to be that

rescue, to be his body, to move for things that matter." Do you agree? Why or why not?

- How is an organization like TWLOHA partnering with God's work of making things on earth the way they are in heaven (see Matthew 6:10)?

Use the space below to write any key points or questions you want to bring to the next group meeting.

session (3)

A GOD TO CALL FATHER

The gospel is powerful enough to bring healing into our relationships with our parents, no matter how jacked up those relationships might be.

Louie Giglio

Orientation

The 1985 movie *Back to the Future* follows high school student Marty McFly as he travels back in time thirty years to 1955. There he meets a teenaged version of his parents and realizes they have many of the same problems and hang-ups that he does. The film is funny, suspenseful, and at times touching. Yet, woven throughout is a profound observation: *Who our parents were really matters.* For good or for ill, the way we were raised makes a mark on our lives, and that mark can continue to affect our relationships in the present.

When you start asking questions about how you were raised, psychologists call it "family of origin" work. And whether it's during a premarital course with your pastor, or in a professional setting with a counselor, at the heart of it are the questions: *Do we believe that things can really change? Does tomorrow have to be the same as today? Does our past, necessarily, have to dictate our present, or can things be different?*

Fortunately for us, God's answer to the question about things being different is always "yes." Our God is a God who acts in this world to change things. That's what he does. This is true for the big things – such as sin and death, where God has acted to defeat them – but it is also true for the relational patterns in our lives. God can bless whatever we inherited from our family of origin, sustain what is healthy, and break the cycles of what is sick.

That's what God does, and it is what this session of *Relat(able)* is all about. How have you been affected by the way you grew up? What did you learn from your parents that was good? What did you learn that was toxic? Furthermore, where does Jesus want to break toxic cycles by inviting you to call God "Father"?

Welcome and Checking In

Go around the group and invite everyone to finish this statement:

My family celebrates birthdays by ____________________.

Last week you were invited to participate in the "Between Sessions" section of the study.

- Did you do one of the activities? If so, which one? If not, why not?
- What are some of the things you wrote down in reflection?
- What did you learn by engaging in these activities?

Hearing the Word

Read aloud in the group 1 John 3:1–11 from The Voice translation. Invite everyone to listen for a fresh insight during the reading.

> [1] *Consider the kind of extravagant love the Father has lav-*
> *ished on us—He calls us children of God! It's true; we are*
> *His beloved children. And in the same way the world didn't*
> *recognize Him, the world does not recognize us either.* [2] *My*
> *loved ones, we have been adopted into God's family; and we*
> *are officially His children now. The full picture of our destiny*
> *is not yet clear, but we know this much: when Jesus appears,*
> *we will be like Him because we will see Him just as He is.* [3] *All*

those who focus their hopes on Him and His coming seek to
purify themselves just as He is pure. [4] *Everyone who lives a life*
of habitual sin is living in moral anarchy. That's what sin is.
[5] *You realize that He came to eradicate sins, that there is not the*
slightest bit of sin in Him. [6] *The ones who live in an intimate*
relationship with Him do not persist in sin, but anyone who
persists in sin has not seen and does not know the real Jesus.
[7] *Children, don't let anyone pull one over on you. The one*
doing the right thing is just imitating Jesus, the Righteous One.
[8] *The one persisting in sin belongs to the diabolical one,*
who has been all about sin from the beginning. That is why
the Son of God came into our world: to destroy the plague
of destruction inflicted on the world by the diabolical one.
[9] *Everyone who has been born into God's family avoids sin as*
a lifestyle because the genes of God's children come from God
Himself. Therefore, a child of God can't live a life of persis-
tent sin. [10] *So it is not hard to figure out who are the children*
of God and who are the children of the diabolical one: those
who lack right standing and those who don't show love for one
another do not belong to God. [11] *The central truth—the one*
you have heard since the beginning of your faith—is that we
must love one another.

Turn to the person next to you and take turns sharing your answers to the following questions:

What does being a child of God mean to you?

Have you ever heard the phrase "a chip off the old block"? What does it mean in your own words?

How does "being a chip off the old block" relate to the passage of Scripture we just read?

Watch the Video

Play the video segment for Session 3. As you watch, use the following outline to record any thoughts or concepts that stand out to you.

Notes

Your ability to relate in the world—the kind of spouse you're going to be, the kind of son or daughter you are today, the kind of friend you are, whether you're datable or not—is wrapped up in the relationship you have with your mom and dad.

The enemy knows God is a perfect Father. If he can fracture relationships with our earthly fathers, he will have put us behind the "eight ball" of fully understanding who God is, how we relate to him, what he thinks about us, and how to live in a relationship with him.

When you come to know Jesus, you receive a new identity. That new identity isn't that you're a church member, or that you believe something, but that you *become* something: a Christian.

You don't have to be afraid of thinking about God as a father. He's not just a bigger version of your dad; he's the version of your dad that you long for deep inside your heart.

We can either reinforce what's been broken in our lives with our mother and father, or we can be part of reversing the curse and leaning into what can be.

The power of the gospel is that we can be the reflection of the love of God to our parents, even if they are not the reflection of the love of God to us.

Group Discussion

Take a few minutes with your group members to discuss what you just watched and explore these concepts in Scripture.

First Impressions

1. Before everyone shares in the large group, turn to one or two people next to you and finish this sentence: "After watching the video, one question I now have is . . ."

Community Reflection

2. Invite everyone to complete the following statement: "I was given my name because . . ."

3. How do you relate to the "God as Father" language in the Bible? Is it helpful to you? Why or why not?

4. What does it mean to "honor your father and mother"?

5. In the video this week, Louie said that we need to honor our parents regardless of what they've done. Do you think he is right about this? How do we honor our father and mother while also telling the truth about the wrong things they might have done?

6. Have you ever seen your relationship with one or both of your parents affect your relationships with others? If so, how? Are these impacts positive or negative or a mixture of each?

7. How can a restored relationship with your mother or father attract others to God? How can it demonstrate the power of God to others?

Becoming Relat(able)

In this session, we have been emphasizing that the way we grew up deeply affects the way we relate to others today. So, for this section, we are going to do a little exercise to reflect on where we have come *from* so we can see where God is taking us *next*. Begin by answering the following questions:

During my childhood, affection was:

a. Shown warmly and often
b. Rarely shown
c. Other: ____________________

During my childhood, anger was:

a. Shown openly and reasonably discussed
b. Not shown—we didn't get angry
c. Dealt with by separating to go and "cool off"—shouting was not accepted
d. Other: ____________________

When my parents disagreed or fought:

a. They yelled and screamed
b. One usually/always gave way to the other
c. They separated to cool off
d. One or both used the "silent treatment"
e. I wouldn't know—they never fought in front of me
f. Other: ______________________

My childhood home was usually:

a. Neat and clean
b. Comfortably cluttered
c. Other: ______________________

In my family, decision making was done by:

a. One parent
b. Both parents in consultation
c. Other: ______________________

In my family, money was:

a. Supposed to be saved and spent only on necessities
b. Not spoken about
c. Used freely for recreational pursuits
d. Other: ______________________

In my family, communication was:

a. Open and free—we all sat around and spoke about our day or our lives
b. Not very open, but we spoke about the important stuff
c. Strained
d. Other: ______________________

Now that you have answered these questions, list in the space below three things you learned about your family of origin that were *healthy*.

Now list three things you learned about your family of origin that were *unhealthy*.

Closing Prayer

Take a moment to allow anyone who would like to do so to share what they have written, and then close the session by inviting everyone to pray. Open the time of prayer with a moment of directed silence in which participants give thanks for the good things they have gleaned from their family of origin. Continue by inviting participants to offer any unhealthy dynamics they inherited from their families to God and ask for his help. (This, again, should be accomplished in a moment of silence.) Finally, conclude by inviting everyone to pray together the prayer that Jesus taught his disciples to pray in Matthew 6:9 – 13:

9 Our Father in heaven,
hallowed be your name,
10 your kingdom come,
your will be done,
on earth as it is in heaven.
11 Give us today our daily bread.
12 And forgive us our debts,
as we also have forgiven our debtors.
13 And lead us not into temptation,
but deliver us from the evil one.

[For yours is the kingdom and the power and the glory forever. Amen.]

BETWEEN-SESSIONS PERSONAL STUDY

Further explore the good news of *Relat(able)* this week by engaging in any or all of the following between-sessions activities. *Be sure to read the reflection questions after each activity and make a few notes in your guide about the experience.* There will be a time to share these reflections at the beginning of the next session.

Love God: Honoring Father and Mother?

Begin by reading the following passage from Exodus 20:1–17:

> 1 *And God spoke all these words:*
> 2 *"I am the* Lord *your God, who brought you out of*
> *Egypt, out of the land of slavery.*
> 3 *"You shall have no other gods before me.*
> 4 *"You shall not make for yourself an image in the form*
> *of anything in heaven above or on the earth beneath or in*
> *the waters below.* 5 *You shall not bow down to them or wor-*
> *ship them; for I, the* Lord *your God, am a jealous God,*

punishing the children for the sin of the parents to the third and fourth generation of those who hate me, 6 *but showing love to a thousand generations of those who love me and keep my commandments.*

7 *"You shall not misuse the name of the LORD your God, for the LORD will not hold anyone guiltless who misuses his name.*

8 *"Remember the Sabbath day by keeping it holy.* 9 *Six days you shall labor and do all your work,* 10 *but the seventh day is a sabbath to the LORD your God. On it you shall not do any work, neither you, nor your son or daughter, nor your male or female servant, nor your animals, nor any foreigner residing in your towns.* 11 *For in six days the LORD made the heavens and the earth, the sea, and all that is in them, but he rested on the seventh day. Therefore the LORD blessed the Sabbath day and made it holy.*

12 *"Honor your father and your mother, so that you may live long in the land the LORD your God is giving you.*

13 *"You shall not murder.*

14 *"You shall not commit adultery.*

15 *"You shall not steal.*

16 *"You shall not give false testimony against your neighbor.*

17 *"You shall not covet your neighbor's house. You shall not covet your neighbor's wife, or his male or female servant, his ox or donkey, or anything that belongs to your neighbor."*

This text comprises the "Ten Commandments" of the Bible, which are described in Exodus 20:1 as words "God spoke." This distinction of these laws coming from something God *said* is significant. God's words here mirror his act of creation in Genesis 1, where he spoke the universe into existence. This means that when God speaks, it is the source of all light and life. For this reason, the Hebrews saw the law as a gift. They were grateful God would show them the way of life, and health, and peace.

All that being said, notice how many of these Ten Commandments include a reference to parents. Two out of the ten mention parents and children—a pretty high percentage. God's words concerning idolatry and his words about honoring parents both speak to generational dynamics, and recognize that sin is something that can be passed on. If we are not careful, we will end up repeating the mistakes of previous generations again and again, and we will end up grooming our own children to also make the same mistakes. This is where the command to honor parents is so brilliant. God knows how sin spreads, but the way to *break* that cycle is not by force, shame, or fear but through *gratitude*.

At first glance, honoring our father and mother is something that sounds naive. It's a nice idea in theory, but given how fractured, dysfunctional, and even abusive our homes can be, who could ever really do this? What's more, isn't a command to honor our parents a way of whitewashing any past or future bad behavior, or even giving bullies *carte blanche* to keep up their violence? The answer is no.

Honoring our parents is about gratitude. Yes, at its best this gratitude flows because of real, tangible acts of love that are demonstrated on a daily basis. However, even if that is not the case, we can still be grateful for our parents because they gave us life. If it were not for "them," there would be no "us." That is something we can appreciate, even if it's the *only* thing.

This open door for gratitude is what breaks the cycle of sin and keeps us from visiting the same pain on others that has been visited on us. Why? Because evil always remakes us in its image. It has a twisted way of forming our hearts and souls to pass on wounds instead of stopping them. Gratitude stops this pattern cold in its tracks. It is the pathway to peace, light, and life. That's why this command is a gift … and is more important today than it's ever been.

- What is one practical way you can honor the parents who gave you life?
- Have you ever seen yourself "pass on" something sad that happened to you to someone else? Explain.
- How can being thankful to God break that cycle?
- What does it mean for you to honor your father and mother?

I'm not a psychiatrist. I'm not a psychologist. I'm not an expert in anything that has to do with anything really, but I am a human being. And I'm pretty well versed in that, and what I've learned about life is when we have significant relationship issues with our mom or dad, it leaves us with deficits in our life. Oh, we may be trying to cover them up or do a "song and dance," but there is stuff not working right on the inside.

Louie Giglio, Relat(able)

Love Yourself: Personal Sabbath

Processing the impact of your family of origin can be tiring work. So for this week's *Love Yourself* exercise, you are reminded that you need to rest. The Sabbath is one of the more powerful yet under obeyed of all the Ten Commandments. Why is that? Part of it can be a lack of self-love. We do not feel as if we deserve the kind of mercy that is at the heart of the Sabbath, so we grind and push on—sometimes until we collapse.

This week, you are invited to break that cycle with rest.

Choose one day this week when you will rest from your labor. This does not mean avoiding all activity—engaging the Sabbath can mean doing active things, but they should be activities that give life and rest, not the completion of work. So go for a hike. Ride your surfboard. Watch a movie. Spend time acting as if the work is done, even if it's not.

If your life is structured so that you cannot rest for a whole day, consider taking smaller chunks of time to start moving toward this goal. Observe a Sabbath from email from 6:00 p.m. until 6:00 a.m. for two days this week. Pick one day to take a nap. Get up earlier one morning and read the paper. Whatever you do, make sure it is life-giving to you because that is, after all, who the Sabbath is for (see Mark 2:27).

Make a few notes about your experience to share with the group next week.

If God can take a broken, fractured, formative relationship, and through you begin to reflect freedom in that relationship, I promise you people are going to stare at you and not be able to take their eyes off of you. They are going to want to know how you did that. And if you succeed in living this out, they're probably going to come to know Jesus.

Louie Giglio, Relat(able)

Love Your Neighbor: Forgiving Your Parents

We all have to forgive our parents. All of us. No matter what. Regardless of how loving or dysfunctional our family was, or how present or absent our parents were, at times we all have to forgive our mom and dad. Part of this is an acknowledgment of the simple reality of sin. Sin is real and its impact cannot be avoided, even in our most important relationships. The other part of this, however, is that the process of forgiveness is the pathway to our freedom.

For this week's *Love Your Neighbor* activity, you are invited to explore the dynamic of parental forgiveness. Use one or more of the articles and links below to wade into this topic:

- Leslie Leyland Fields, "Forgiving Our Fathers and Mothers," *Today's Christian Woman,* http://www.todayschristianwoman.com/articles/2014/september-week-4/forgiving-our-fathers-and-mothers.html. Leslie also wrote an award-winning book on this topic – see her website leslieleylandfields.com for more information. Or read an interview with her at http://

jonathanmerritt.religionnews.com/2014/02/13/forgive-parents-interview-leslie-leyland-fields/.
- Dr. Linda Mintle, "How to Handle Conflict with Your Parents," *Relevant,* http://www.relevantmagazine.com/life/how-handle-conflict-your-parents. In this article, Dr. Mintle offers insights on what it means to honor your parents, even when you don't agree with them.

After reading these articles, consider the following questions:

- What things in your life are you grateful to your parents for?
- In what areas of your life do you need to forgive your parents?
- Are there any cycles in your life that you want to break? If so, what are they?
- How can forgiving your parents set you free?

Use the space below to write any key points or questions you want to bring to the next group meeting.

session (4)

THE FRIEND EVERYONE LONGS FOR

Somebody is going to get the benefit of getting a friend that they want in life, because it's going to be you.

Louie Giglio

Orientation

Take a moment to think about one of your best friends. Not an acquaintance, but someone whose friendship is deep and with whom you have history. Lots of images will probably come to mind as you do this. You may think about who your friend is, where your friend is from, and how the two of you met. You will recall the memories of special moments you have shared and events you have attended together. You might also think about when you are going to see this friend next and what the two of you will do.

One of the things that probably did not come to mind—but is true nonetheless—is that this friend is also someone with whom you have had conflict. The people we are closest to in this life are usually the people with whom we have fought. Think about it. Your closest friends are those with whom you have had it out, but then, at some point, worked through that conflict together. That makes your friend someone whom you have had to forgive or who has forgiven you.

This dynamic of forgiveness is what makes our friendships strong. It is one of the mysteries and hopes of Christian relationships. In Christ, conflict is not a deal breaker but a path to depth and intimacy. That's how it works. God is so good that he is able to work even our relational failings toward something redemptive.

But we have to do our part, which is what this session of *Relat(able)* is all about. What kind of friend do we want to be? How do we handle conflict? What does it look like to work with God to guide even our broken relationships toward redemption? Answering these questions will open us up to

God working in our lives and relationships, and it can make us the kind of friends everyone longs for.

Welcome and Checking In

Go around the group and invite everyone to answer the following questions:

> Who was your best friend when you were growing up?
>
> What did you both do together?

Last week you were invited to participate in the "Between Sessions" section of the study.

- Did you do one of the activities? If so, which one? If not, why not?
- What are some of the things you wrote down in reflection?
- What did you learn by engaging in these activities?

Hearing the Word

Read Romans 12:9–21 aloud in the group. Invite everyone to listen for a fresh insight during the reading.

> 9 *Love must be sincere. Hate what is evil; cling to what is*
> *good.* 10 *Be devoted to one another in love. Honor one another*
> *above yourselves.* 11 *Never be lacking in zeal, but keep your*

spiritual fervor, serving the Lord. [12] *Be joyful in hope, patient*
in affliction, faithful in prayer. [13] *Share with the Lord's people*
who are in need. Practice hospitality.

[14] *Bless those who persecute you; bless and do not curse.*
[15] *Rejoice with those who rejoice; mourn with those who*
mourn. [16] *Live in harmony with one another. Do not be*
proud, but be willing to associate with people of low position.
Do not be conceited.

[17] *Do not repay anyone evil for evil. Be careful to do what*
is right in the eyes of everyone. [18] *If it is possible, as far as it*
depends on you, live at peace with everyone. [19] *Do not take*
revenge, my dear friends, but leave room for God's wrath, for
it is written: "It is mine to avenge; I will repay," says the Lord.
[20] *On the contrary: "If your enemy is hungry, feed him; if he*
is thirsty, give him something to drink. In doing this, you will
heap burning coals on his head."

[21] *Do not be overcome by evil, but overcome evil with*
good.

Turn to the person next to you and take turns sharing your answers to the following questions:

For you, what is the most challenging part of this passage of Scripture?

What do you think it means to bless someone? How about blessing those who persecute you . . . what does that look like?

How does the call to "not be overcome by evil, but overcome evil with good" play out in a violent world?

Watch the Video

Play the video segment for Session 4. As you watch, use the following outline to record any thoughts or concepts that stand out to you.

Notes

Getting married is not about finding the perfect woman or finding the perfect man. It's about becoming the person that God wants you to be.

For us to become the person we want our friends to be, the first challenge is to become a "one-faced friend," with no hidden agendas.

The second challenge for us is to be friends who extinguish evil and celebrate good. We want to be the kind of friends who do not allow small things to escalate into relationship-breaking events.

Our third challenge is to be friends who are open-handed—friends who share what we have with those who are hurting and in need.

The fourth challenge is to be friends who can rise above the fray. We can choose to politely decline the invitation to get into a fight and go on about our business.

The fifth challenge is to be friends who are there for others during the good times and the bad.

The sixth challenge is to be friends who—as far as it depends on us—live at peace with one another.

Group Discussion

Take a few minutes with your group members to discuss what you just watched and explore these concepts in Scripture.

First Impressions

1. Before everyone shares in the large group, turn to one or two people next to you and finish this sentence: "After watching the video, one question I now have is …"

Community Reflection

2. When was the last conflict you were involved in? Can you share what caused it?

3. What "gets your goat" when you are at odds with a friend or family member? Is there anything that tempts you to be an escalator of conflict?

4. What are some strategies you could employ that de-escalate conflict?

5. What is the difference between being a person "who lives at peace with everyone" and a person who is a doormat?

6. What are things that small groups (like this one) can do to, as Louie suggests, "share with those in need and practice hospitality"?

7. If God could do one thing in your life to empower you to "live at peace with everyone," what would you want it to be?

Becoming Relat(able)

In the video, Louie lists six things that make a great friend. They are:

1. A one-faced friend
2. A de-escalator of conflict
3. Someone who is open-handed, generous, and hospitable
4. Someone who rises above the fray
5. A person who floats freely between everyone (joining us at the party and at our lowest points)
6. A peacemaker

As a group, review the list and define each characteristic based on what you remember from the video. Then invite the group members to share which of these items they already practice in their friendships and which one they would most like God to grow in their life.

Closing Prayer

Finally, conclude by inviting everyone to pray together the prayer that Jesus taught his disciples to pray in Matthew 6:9–13:

> *[9] Our Father in heaven,*
> *hallowed be your name,*
> *[10] your kingdom come,*
> *your will be done,*
> *on earth as it is in heaven.*
> *[11] Give us today our daily bread.*
> *[12] And forgive us our debts,*
> *as we also have forgiven our debtors.*
> *[13] And lead us not into temptation,*
> *but deliver us from the evil one.*
>
> *[For yours is the kingdom and the power*
> *and the glory forever. Amen.]*

BETWEEN-SESSIONS PERSONAL STUDY

Further explore the good news of *Relat(able)* this week by engaging in any or all of the following between-sessions activities. *Be sure to read the reflection questions after each activity and make a few notes in your guide about the experience.* There will be a time to share these reflections at the beginning of the next session.

Love God: Be a One-Faced Friend

Louie suggests that healthy friendships start with God's love and approval. His image is that of a one-faced friend, not a two-faced friend. Louie says we will never be a one-faced friend if we don't get the shovel of God's approval—if we don't agree with God that we're somebody of great worth or we aren't starting to repair our core relationships in life. The reason why we become a two-faced friend is because we want acceptance from people. So we tell one person one thing and tell another person something else simply because we are trying to bolster our position in the situation.

For this week's *Love God* section, read the following Bible verses and reflect on what each says about God's love for and approval of you: Psalm 86:15; Zephaniah 3:17; Matthew 6:25–34; Romans 8:37–39; and Ephesians 2:4–5.

- Which of these verses from the Bible taught you the most about God's love?
- Were any hard to accept? Why?
- How can this kind of love empower you to be a "one-faced" friend?

We don't want to be friends who sweep things under the rug. We want to speak truth and love to our friends. We want to deal with our friends in reality. We don't want to be friends who escalate situations for our own personal gain—which is why we escalate things in the first place.

Louie Giglio, Relat(able)

Love Yourself: Get Some Sleep

How many conflicts have you seen in the office, classroom, or home where one of the participants ultimately admitted, "I'm just tired"? Have you ever lost your temper because you were sleep deprived and worn out? Most people have. That's because sleep is a crucial part of our health that we often neglect. Therefore, as a way to love yourself this week, your activity is to get some more ... sleep!

Pick two or three nights this week and go to bed an hour earlier than you normally do. This may involve sacrificing a TV program or video game, but the discipline will be worth it. Arrange your life so that you can complete your day earlier and get a full hour of extra sleep.

Then, on the mornings after your extra sleep, consider what it does to your mood, your joy, your patience, your choices, and your ability to be present to those around you. Also, evaluate your ability to be the kind of friend that Louie describes. Of the list he offers in the video, consider if any of these came easier when you were more rested.

1. Was I a better one-faced friend?
2. Did I de-escalate conflict?
3. Did I take any opportunities to be open-handed, generous, and hospitable?
4. What was my capacity for empathy and celebration?
5. Did I notice any opportunities to make peace?

Make a few notes about your experience to share with the group next week.

The gospel doesn't treat people differently based on what part of town they live in, or what socioeconomic stratum they might currently be in, or what their family history is, or anything else about them. The gospel highlights and dignifies every single person on planet Earth. It lifts up every person equally into the presence of God. Therefore, we should want to be the kind of people who are easy-moving—up and down, side to side—among all kinds of people.

Louie Giglio, Relat(able)

Love Your Neighbor: What Kind of Friend Am I?

For this week's *Love Your Neighbor* activity, you are invited to consider what kind of friend you are to others. Read one of the three articles below from *Relevant* magazine to wade into this topic:

- Drew Brown, "What Keeps Us from Having Deeper Friendships," http://www.relevantmagazine.com/life/what-keeps-us-having-deeper-friendships
- Bethany Shaeffer, "When Your Friendships Need an Overhaul," http://www.relevantmagazine.com/life/when-your-friendships-need-overhaul
- "Lasting Friendships," http://www.relevantmagazine.com/life/relationship/features/1714-lasting-friendships

After reading these resources, consider the following questions:

- What are two ways I am a great friend?
- What are two ways I might be a draining friend?
- What is something I want God to do in me in order to make me the kind of friend everyone longs for?

Use the space below to write any key points or questions you want to bring to the next group meeting.

session (5)

BECOMING SOMEONE VS. FINDING SOMEONE

God knows that ultimately what you need most is not a mate but a Maker.

Louie Giglio

Orientation

On the wall of a fitness center was a poster jammed with fifty different inspirational clichés. "Don't stop when you're tired; stop when you're done." "You don't have to be great to start, but you have to start to be great." "Tough times don't last; tough people do." These phrases, among others, were all overlapping each other to make a collage-like piece of artwork. Most of the phrases were things you would expect to see in the gym, except for one. In the bottom right corner was the phrase "Be the change you want to see in the world." It's not a cliché often used for exercise.

Now, the way clichés become clichés is that they take an authentic nugget of wisdom and overuse it until it becomes trite and meaningless. The thing that is hard to remember about clichés is that there is an underlying truth to them. This is what enables them to endure. Clichés are clichés only because they connect to something that's actual and authentic. This is probably why "Be the change you want to see in the world" was on the poster at the fitness center. It is a call for each of us to take personal responsibility for the inner work required in order to effect outward change. Making a difference, then, begins not by fixating on the problems *out there* but instead by looking *in here*, to one's own life, and making changes there first. That dynamic is what this session of *Relat(able)* is all about.

This week, Louie invites us to shift our expectations when it comes to being in a relationship. In our passion to find contentment in general or a mate in particular, we fixate on finding what we're looking for *out there*. Louie suggests that when we do this, we might actually miss what God wants to do in us—*in here*. It seems that, whether it is cliché or not, the things we most want to see changed in our lives still start with looking inward.

The question is, *Do you believe this?* Does this sound like good news to you or not? Consider this as we dive into Louie's invitation to *become* someone instead of spending all our energy trying to *find* someone—and let's see what God does next.

Welcome and Checking In

Go around the group and invite everyone to answer the following question:

What was your favorite book when you were young?

Last week you were invited to participate in the "Between Sessions" section of the study.

- Did you do one of the activities? If so, which one? If not, why not?
- What are some of the things you wrote down in reflection?
- What did you learn by engaging in these activities?

Hearing the Word

Read Matthew 6:25–34 aloud in the group. Invite everyone to listen for a fresh insight during the reading.

> *25 Therefore I tell you, do not worry about your life, what you will eat or drink; or about your body, what you will wear. Is not life more than food, and the body more than clothes?*
> *26 Look at the birds of the air; they do not sow or reap or store away in barns, and yet your heavenly Father feeds them. Are you not much more valuable than they? 27 Can any one of you by worrying add a single hour to your life?*
>
> *28 And why do you worry about clothes? See how the flowers of the field grow. They do not labor or spin. 29 Yet I tell you that not even Solomon in all his splendor was dressed like one of these. 30 If that is how God clothes the grass of the field, which is here today and tomorrow is thrown into the fire, will he not much more clothe you—you of little faith?*
> *31 So do not worry, saying, "What shall we eat?" or "What shall we drink?" or "What shall we wear?" 32 For the pagans run after all these things, and your heavenly Father knows that you need them. 33 But seek first his kingdom and his righteousness, and all these things will be given to you as well. 34 Therefore do not worry about tomorrow, for tomorrow will worry about itself. Each day has enough trouble of its own.*

Turn to the person next to you and take turns sharing your answers to the following questions:

> What about these words of Jesus sounds like "good news" to you?

What do you think it means to "seek first [God's] kingdom and [God's] righteousness"?

What responsibility do we bear for taking care of ourselves while still depending on God as Jesus instructs?

Watch the Video

Play the video segment for Session 5. As you watch, use the following outline to record any thoughts or concepts that stand out to you.

Notes

Singleness can bring with it a lot of anxiety, and over time that anxiety can become crippling for us. We need God to alleviate that anxiety and plant hope in our hearts.

The first seed of hope is knowing that we have a Father who promises that if we prioritize a life of seeking him, he will prioritize a life of providing for us.

The second seed of hope is that what we ultimately need most is not a *mate* but a *Maker*. Before we fall in love with a mate, we need to fall in love with our Maker.

The third seed of hope is that even though we can't control whether or not we *find* someone, we can control *becoming* someone.

The fourth seed of hope is that God is in the business of moving us toward the proximity of the person he wants us to meet.

The fifth seed of hope is that there is power in today. We can't allow the enemy to steal who God wants us to become today by causing us to stress about a potential outcome tomorrow.

Group Discussion

Take a few minutes with your group members to discuss what you just watched and explore these concepts in Scripture.

First Impressions

1. Before everyone shares in the large group, turn to one or two people next to you and finish this sentence: "After watching the video, one question I now have is …"

Community Reflection

2. Louie says he is dealing with some touchy subjects. Was there anything in his teaching that challenged you or even rubbed you the wrong way? If so, what?

3. What do you find yourself worrying about more: the past or the future?

4. Louie says the trick is shifting our priority from finding somebody to becoming someone. What do you think this means after seeing the video? How do we do this?

5. Louie proposes that the seed of hope for all our relationships – married or single – is planted in knowing that we have a Father who promises that if we will prioritize a life of seeking him, then he will prioritize a life of providing for us. This is amazing news, but it can be hard to trust. Is it hard or easy for you to trust God with all of your relationships? Why did you answer the way you did?

6. Louie says that marriages stay together when both people are moving toward Jesus. Why does this bring a couple together? How have you found this to be true?

7. In Romans 8:24 – 26, Paul writes, *"For in this hope we were saved. But hope that is seen is no hope at all. Who hopes for what they already have? But if we hope for what we do not yet have, we wait for it patiently. In the same way, the Spirit helps us in our weakness. We do not know what we ought to pray for, but the Spirit himself intercedes for us through wordless groans."* If the Holy Spirit helps you hope where you can't hope yourself, where do you most need that hope in your own process of becoming relatable?

Becoming Relat(able)

For this activity, each participant will need an 8½ x 11 sheet of paper.

This week's "Becoming Relat(able)" section invites us to step deeper into one of Louie's seeds of hope. In the video today, Louie identifies his fourth seed of hope as understanding God's rhythm. What he means is that when we give ourselves, our trust, and our energy to God, and submit to God's molding of us, God takes care of our other relational needs. Our hope is not in finding the right person but in being loved by God. That means we don't need to go looking for anything, because we already have God's love. We just need to accept that beautiful fact.

Invite everyone in the group to take a piece of paper. Then, instruct the group to fold their paper, and slowly crease every fold. People can fold it into a random shape, a paper airplane, or fancy origami. Whatever they choose, just be clear that this is not random "wadding" but an act of intention.

With every crease, invite group members to reflect on the ways they most want to be shaped by God. Let the activity be a way of saying yes to God's invitation to *become* someone instead of *finding* someone.

Where do you need God to shape, sculpt, and form you?

Closing Prayer

Close by inviting the group to silently pray for the person on their left to become who God is making them to be. Then, invite them to pray for the person on their right to have the hope that comes from seeking God's kingdom first.

BETWEEN-SESSIONS PERSONAL STUDY

Further explore the good news of *Relat(able)* this week by engaging in any or all of the following between-sessions activities. *Be sure to read the reflection questions after each activity and make a few notes in your guide about the experience.* There will be a time to share these reflections at the beginning of the next session.

Love God: The Sacrament of Singleness

Begin by reading the following passage from Luke 20:27–40:

> *27 Some of the Sadducees, who say there is no resurrection,*
> *came to Jesus with a question. 28 "Teacher," they said, "Moses*
> *wrote for us that if a man's brother dies and leaves a wife but*
> *no children, the man must marry the widow and raise up off-*
> *spring for his brother. 29 Now there were seven brothers. The*
> *first one married a woman and died childless. 30 The second*
> *31 and then the third married her, and in the same way the*
> *seven died, leaving no children. 32 Finally, the woman died*

too. [33] Now then, at the resurrection whose wife will she be,
since the seven were married to her?"

[34] Jesus replied, "The people of this age marry and are
given in marriage. [35] But those who are considered worthy of
taking part in the age to come and in the resurrection from
the dead will neither marry nor be given in marriage, [36] and
they can no longer die; for they are like the angels. They are
God's children, since they are children of the resurrection.
[37] But in the account of the burning bush, even Moses showed
that the dead rise, for he calls the Lord 'the God of Abraham,
and the God of Isaac, and the God of Jacob.' [38] He is not the
God of the dead, but of the living, for to him all are alive."

[39] Some of the teachers of the law responded, "Well said,
teacher!" [40] And no one dared to ask him any more questions.

One of the most audacious claims of the Christian faith is that after all is said and done, those who follow Christ will live together with God in his new heaven and new earth (see Revelation 21–22). We will have new bodies, just like Jesus himself (see Acts 24:14–15 and 1 Corinthians 15). This is a hope that was incubated by the Old Testament prophets yet remained contentious in Jesus' day. That's what the exchange between Jesus and the Sadducees is about in Luke 20:27–40. The Sadducees did not believe in the resurrection, so in an attempt to trap and mock Jesus, they constructed a scenario about marriage and remarriage born from the Hebrew law (see Deuteronomy 25:5–10).

Bad idea.

What Jesus does with the Sadducees' questions amazes everyone. He subverts their whole line of questioning by stating that marriage is not something that lasts into God's new world. It is a temporary arrangement that is part of only this age. The implications of this are vast and far-reaching, but it has two interesting applications for you this week.

First, marriage is a picture. Some Christian traditions call this picture a sacrament, or say marriage has sanctity, but what they are getting at is that marriage points to something larger than itself. It points to the way things are supposed to be. Marriage, at its best, is a picture of Christ's relationship to the church (see Matthew 25:1–13; Ephesians 5:25; and Revelation 22:16–17). It is a witness of God's Genesis dream of wholeness between all people and God.

This means if marriage is a picture, then singleness is a picture too. If marriage is a signpost pointing to the way relationships are *supposed* to be in this age, then singleness is the signpost showing what they are actually *going* to be in the age to come. In God's new world, Jesus says there is no giving and receiving in marriage because things are as they are meant to be again. We don't need the *picture* anymore because we can now see and experience the *real thing*. In God's new world we are all in community with one another, and if there is a marriage, it is our relationship as the church to Jesus himself, the bridegroom.

You can see why the crowds were amazed at Jesus' teaching, while the Sadducees were scandalized. Which one are you? Consider this audacious reality as you reflect on the following questions:

- If you are married, in what ways can your marriage, and the way you live it out, be a witness of God's dream for this world?
- If you are single, in what ways can your singleness, and the way you live it out, be a picture of God's new world?

- How can the church honor the sacramental witness of both marriage and singleness? What does it mean that only one of these two states lasts into God's new world?

Make a few notes about your experience to share with the group next week.

It's not God's nature to not give you what you need. But it is God's desire that you seek him above those needs. Therefore, you shouldn't worry about tomorrow and what your spouse's name is, or when you're going to meet that person, or where you will live, or what your wedding day is going to look like, or where you're going to go on your honeymoon, or what kind of job you're going to have, or how many kids you're going to have. Don't worry about tomorrow.

Louie Giglio, Relat(able)

Love Yourself: The Lord's Prayer

One of the most powerful yet challenging parts of Louie's teaching in this session is his call for inner reflection. At every turn, Louie reminds us that what we're looking for starts by entrusting ourselves to God and God's desire for us. We are to stop asking, "What's my type?" and start asking, "What type am I?" When we ask this question, and trust God to guide us into the answer, we find the hope and peace of the kingdom.

The section of the Sermon on the Mount from which Louie teaches is preceded by this teaching from Jesus on prayer (Matthew 6:5 – 13):

> 5 *And when you pray, do not be like the hypocrites, for they*
> *love to pray standing in the synagogues and on the street cor-*
> *ners to be seen by others. Truly I tell you, they have received*
> *their reward in full.* 6 *But when you pray, go into your room,*
> *close the door and pray to your Father, who is unseen. Then*
> *your Father, who sees what is done in secret, will reward you.*
> 7 *And when you pray, do not keep on babbling like pagans,*
> *for they think they will be heard because of their many words.*
> 8 *Do not be like them, for your Father knows what you need*
> *before you ask him.*
>
> 9 *This, then, is how you should pray:*
> *Our Father in heaven,*
> *hallowed be your name,*
> 10 *your kingdom come,*
> *your will be done,*
> *on earth as it is in heaven.*
> 11 *Give us today our daily bread.*
> 12 *And forgive us our debts,*
> *as we also have forgiven our debtors.*
> 13 *And lead us not into temptation,*
> *but deliver us from the evil one.*

In this prayer, Jesus invites us to entrust ourselves fully to God. He invites us to receive forgiveness for our sins. This has to do with our past. He invites us to ask for daily bread. This has to do with our present. Finally, he instructs us to pray that we will not be led into temptation. This has to do with our future.

In this way, the Lord's Prayer becomes a vehicle for entrusting all of life—past, present, and future—to God. It also means that his teaching about worry (found earlier in this session in "Hearing the Word") is directly connected to the prayer. It's Jesus' way of showing us what happens when we don't entrust ourselves to God: we become consumed with worry and anxiety.

Your invitation in *Love Yourself* this week is to pray the Lord's Prayer every time a moment of worry, stress, or anxiety hits you regarding your relationships. Let the prayer function as a tool for trusting all of yourself to God. He is trustworthy and will take care of all you need.

Make a few notes about your experience to share with the group next week.

Our happiness is rooted in a Father who sees what we need and is able to provide those things at just the right time.... So, we don't worry about tomorrow, because we have a Father who promises that if we prioritize a life of seeking him, he will prioritize a life of providing for us.

Louie Giglio, Relat(able)

Love Your Neighbor: Stop Being Afraid to Fail

In the video this week, we discussed that one of the reasons why trusting God with our relationship futures is so hard is because the prospect of failing is so paralyzing. To explore this further, do a web search for "Conan O'Brien's 2011 Dartmouth College Commencement Address" and watch the entire speech (or just the culled highlights you can find online).

O'Brien gave this speech the year after he was promised the *Tonight Show* and then had it taken from him by the network. In the speech, he muses on why having your worst fear realized is the most liberating thing that can happen to a person. It is full of humor and profound insights and connects to this week's topic in the way it invites us to stop worrying all the time. Our anxiety will not function as a magic talisman to ward off tragedy. God is the only one who can truly take care of us, and he alone is the one we should trust.

After you watch the video, consider the following questions:

- What was the most helpful part of O'Brien's remarks for you?
- How does this message relate to Louie's message and our topic this week?
- How easy or hard is it for you to trust God, even with your failures?

Use the space below to write any key points or questions you want to bring to the next group meeting.

session (6)

HANDSHAKE OF PEACE

The cross is the template for reconciliation in the relationships of our lives.

Louie Giglio

Orientation

When was the last time you were kissed in church? It's been a while, hasn't it? Why would this question even be asked? Well, in no less than four places in the New Testament, Christians are instructed to "greet one aother with a holy kiss" (Romans 16:16; 1 Corinthians 16:20; 2 Corinthians 13:12; and 1 Thessalonians 5:26). So, what are you waiting for? Next Sunday, it's time to pucker up. Unless, of course, there is something else going on here.

In the earliest days of the church, Christians participated in a ritual act called "passing the peace." Through this ritual, Christians would affirm and actualize their reconciled relationships before receiving Holy Communion. And if anyone had a broken relationship or unforgiveness in his or her heart, that person was expected to work it out during the passing of the peace, lest he or she receive the sacrament in an unworthy manner.

The action that Christians would use to "pass the peace" in these early days was kissing each other. This is what the holy kiss meant and, what's more, it was an act that affected what it symbolized. When you engaged the kiss of peace, you proclaimed and made reconciliation happen. For our final session of *Relat(able)*, we will explore what it looks like to take these first steps toward reconciliation. We will look at how we do this, when we do this, and why we would want to do this.

The Bible reminds us that reconciliation is possible, and references to the kiss of peace witness its necessity. We still have rituals today that embody what the kiss of peace symbolized, such as the shaking of hands to close a deal. Louie builds on this symbol this week by inviting us to consider how we might extend not the kiss, but the handshake of peace.

Welcome and Checking In

Go around the group and invite everyone to answer the following question:

> Who is your favorite fictional villain? (The character can be from film, literature, or television.)

Last week you were invited to participate in the "Between Sessions" section of the study.

- Did you do one of the activities? If so, which one? If not, why not?
- What are some of the things you wrote down in reflection?
- What did you learn by engaging in these activities?

Hearing the Word

Read Romans 12:9–21 aloud in the group. Invite everyone to listen for a fresh insight during the reading.

> [9] *Love must be sincere. Hate what is evil; cling to what is*
> *good.* [10] *Be devoted to one another in love. Honor one another*
> *above yourselves.* [11] *Never be lacking in zeal, but keep your*
> *spiritual fervor, serving the Lord.* [12] *Be joyful in hope, patient*

in affliction, faithful in prayer. 13 *Share with the Lord's people*
who are in need. Practice hospitality.

14 *Bless those who persecute you; bless and do not curse.*
15 *Rejoice with those who rejoice; mourn with those who mourn.*
16 *Live in harmony with one another. Do not be proud, but*
be willing to associate with people of low position. Do not
be conceited.

17 *Do not repay anyone evil for evil. Be careful to do what*
is right in the eyes of everyone. 18 *If it is possible, as far as it*
depends on you, live at peace with everyone. 19 *Do not take*
revenge, my dear friends, but leave room for God's wrath, for
it is written: "It is mine to avenge; I will repay," says the Lord.
20 *On the contrary: "If your enemy is hungry, feed him; if he*
is thirsty, give him something to drink. In doing this, you will
heap burning coals on his head."

21 *Do not be overcome by evil, but overcome evil with*
good.

Turn to the person next to you and take turns sharing your answers to the following questions:

Louie worked out of this same Scripture passage in Session 4. Did you hear anything new this time around as a result of what you have learned during this study?

What does it mean to you to "live in harmony with one another"?

Can Paul's call to "hate what is evil; cling to what is good" and to "live in harmony" go together? If so, how? If not, why not?

Watch the Video

Play the video segment for Session 6. As you watch, use the following outline to record any thoughts or concepts that stand out to you.

Notes

The question is whether we are able—as the people of God—to think about restoration coming into *all* of our relationships that are broken and fractured.

The cross was the place where God Almighty brokered a deal. And the terms of that deal were *my Son for you, because I want peace with you.*

The cross of Jesus is the template by which reconciliation happens in our relationships with each other.

As Christians, we are the people who seek the possibility of peace. It's not natural for people to want reconciliation, but we are supernatural because we are now alive by faith.

If we want to stand out in life, all we have to do is go the second mile—because there is no traffic in that lane.

The power that makes it possible for reconciliation to come in shattered relationships, where wrongs have been done and people have been hurt, is the Holy Spirit of God.

Group Discussion

Take a few minutes with your group members to discuss what you just watched and explore these concepts in Scripture.

First Impressions

1. Before everyone shares in the large group, turn to one or two people next to you and finish this sentence: "After watching the video, one question I now have is ..."

Community Reflection

2. Louie talks this week about relationships between people being restored. What's the difference between forgiveness and reconciliation?

3. Do you think the Bible's definition of peace is different from the world's definition? Why or why not?

4. In Romans 12:18, Paul says, "If it is possible, as far as it depends on you, live at peace with everyone." How do you know when peace is *not* possible anymore?

5. Louie says that the agent of peace is the Holy Spirit. What does he mean by this?

6. Why is leaving the results of reconciliation with God the best, and hardest, thing to do?

Becoming Relat(able)

For this activity, you will need a bucket of water and enough small stones for every person in the group to have one.

Forgiveness is a beautiful but nuanced affair. It is not the same thing as reconciliation, though it begins that process. It is not the same thing as saying, "It's okay," because you have to call sin what it is to authentically forgive it. It also does not mean there are no consequences or legal ramifications, because sometimes the people we need to forgive also need to go to jail. What forgiveness is, in essence, is letting go of the burden that has been thrown in your lap by someone's sin against you.

When you are wronged by someone, you get a wound that you have to carry around. Forgiveness occurs when you decide to stop carrying that wound around and let it go. As such, forgiveness only takes one person, which is how it is different from reconciliation. Reconciliation takes two people and may not be possible. Forgiveness does not, and it is therefore always possible, because it all starts and stops with you.

The process of forgiving can be described in three steps: (1) name it, (2) shame it, and (3) let it go. First, we name what happened to us: "She took the money and ran." "He was unfaithful." Whatever it was, we tell the truth about it and do not pull punches. Second, we shame it. Shaming the sin means saying that what happened was not okay. Definitively. We call it out and declare that what happened to us was wrong while also describing why it was wrong. But then, third, instead of getting revenge or demanding payback from our offender, we let it go. We release our debtor of the debt he or she owes us. We drop it and send it away.

For today's "Becoming Relat(able)" exercise, consider a person with whom you want to be at peace. Next, consider if there is anything you need to forgive to make that possible. On the table in front of you is a small pile of stones and a bucket of water. Take a stone, and while you hold it in your hand, let it become associated with the wrong that you want to forgive. Take as long as you need and squeeze the stone tight to express any pain it has caused you.

As you hold the stone, *name* the wrong that you want to forgive, and *shame* it by saying it was not okay. Then, when you are ready, hold the stone out over the bucket and *let it go*. Let this process of letting it go be an invitation to God to move in your heart and free you from the burden of this debt as you forgive your debtor.

Pray. God is near.

Once everyone has finished the reflection, invite anyone who would like to share with the group what God has done or what he or she hopes God will do. Conclude by using the following prompts to close out your group time for *Relat(able)*:

- Fill in the blanks in the following sentences: Because of my *Relat(able)* experience, I used to think ___________, but now I know ___________.
- The best thing about this experience was ___________. The hardest thing was ___________________.
- At the beginning of this study, you were invited to reflect on which one of three relationships you wanted God to grow you in the most: your relationship with God, your relationship with yourself, or your relationship with others. Did you grow in one of these areas? Why or why not? What do you want God to do next?

Closing Prayer

End the meeting by inviting everyone in the group to pray silently for the person on his or her left. Pray that this person will become more and more relat(able) as God works all things in his or her life toward his good purposes!

PERSONAL STUDY FOR THE COMING DAYS

Further explore the good news of *Relat(able)* this week by engaging in any or all of the following activities. *Be sure to read the reflection questions after each activity and make a few notes in your guide about the experience.* Consider sharing your reflections with a fellow group member or close friend sometime soon.

Love God: Getting Out of the "Good Business" Business

Begin by reading the following passage from Matthew 18:23–35:

> [23] *Therefore, the kingdom of heaven is like a king who wanted*
> *to settle accounts with his servants.* [24] *As he began the settle-*
> *ment, a man who owed him ten thousand bags of gold was*
> *brought to him.* [25] *Since he was not able to pay, the master*
> *ordered that he and his wife and his children and all that he*
> *had be sold to repay the debt.*

26 At this the servant fell on his knees before him. "Be
patient with me," he begged, "and I will pay back every-
thing." 27 The servant's master took pity on him, canceled the
debt and let him go.

28 But when that servant went out, he found one of his
fellow servants who owed him a hundred silver coins. He
grabbed him and began to choke him. "Pay back what you
owe me!" he demanded.

29 His fellow servant fell to his knees and begged him, "Be
patient with me, and I will pay it back."

30 But he refused. Instead, he went off and had the man
thrown into prison until he could pay the debt. 31 When the
other servants saw what had happened, they were outraged
and went and told their master everything that had happened.

32 Then the master called the servant in. "You wicked ser-
vant," he said, "I canceled all that debt of yours because you
begged me to. 33 Shouldn't you have had mercy on your fellow
servant just as I had on you?" 34 In anger his master handed
him over to the jailers to be tortured, until he should pay back
all he owed.

35 This is how my heavenly Father will treat each of you
unless you forgive your brother or sister from your heart.

This is one of Jesus' most powerful and provocative parables. He tells it to illustrate his response to the question, "How many times do I have to forgive people who sin against me?" Jesus says forgiveness should always be a possibility, and this story about masters, slaves, and unpayable debts is intended to help his hearers appropriate the tough teaching.

To get at the beauty of this parable, let's start with the king who settles his accounts. Like a good businessman, he has a ledger with a record of everyone whom he owes and who owes him. Everything is logged and tracked in his book.

What kicks the parable into gear, however, is when the king decides to call in all his outstanding debts. Everyone to whom he has loaned money must pay. Now. One slave owes an astronomical debt, so big that it is more than he could ever pay off in a hundred lifetimes. Jesus makes it this large to prove a point: the slave's insistence that he will pay it back is laughable. He never could. But that's not what sways the king to have mercy on him. The king is swayed only by his own pity. He is fundamentally softhearted, and expects this man whom he has forgiven to be the same.

Unfortunately, the forgiven slave immediately goes out and puts the screws to someone who owes him a small amount of money. When the king learns of this, he calls the slave back in. He cannot understand why this man would not show mercy as he was shown mercy, and thus the king hands him over to the jailers to be tortured.

But the story's meaning is deeper still.

Consider the role of the king. If his business is owed a large sum of money, and he says the debtor does not have to pay it, then is that good or bad for business? Right. It's terrible for the bottom line, the shareholders, and the fourth-quarter profits. Yet that's what the king decides to do. When he forgives the huge debt, it's as if he closes his book and decides he is no longer living by the ledger. He has stopped being in the "good business" business.

By contrast, consider the unforgiving slave. While the king closes his book and stops the living-by-the-ledger system, the unforgiving slave does not. He holds onto his book and is determined to live by it. That's the problem Jesus is illustrating.

The ledger system is toxic. It can function only in a system where there is no mercy.

The ledger system requires that you pay everyone you owe, and everyone who owes you pays you. Think about that. What if you made a list of every bad thing you ever did? And what if everybody else did too? And what if you made a list of every wrong that's ever been done to you? And everybody else did too? And then, what if everyone set out to make each other pay—no matter what, and with no mercy? Such an existence would be torture.

That's Jesus' point. Living by the books is torture, which is why God doesn't do it. And just as we don't want God to keep a list when it comes to our shortcomings, why do we think it's a good idea to keep a list of other people's shortcomings? Jesus is inviting us to get out of the "good business" business too.

So, what do you think? What will you do with *your* book? Consider the following:

- Where are you living by the ledger system?
- Is it harder to receive mercy or to give mercy? Why?
- What is the difference between granting forgiveness and enabling destructive behavior?
- How can we not live by the ledger system yet still hold people accountable for their actions?

God Almighty decided there was going to be peace. And he didn't do it because his borders were threatened. He didn't do it because he needed an economic advantage in the world. He didn't need open trade markets. He didn't need a political alliance. There was nothing in it for him other than the fact that he really did want to have a relationship with you and me, and because he was just and holy. Peace had to be made, and it had a price to be paid so that we could be freed forever. On the cross a deal was brokered when Christ willingly stepped into the story, and peace was made between heaven and earth.

Louie Giglio, Relat(able)

Love Yourself: Build the Bridge

In this week's session, Louie invites us to consider which relationships in our life have friction, and what it would take to reconcile them. This is a challenging proposition, and, as he admits, for many reasons (including safety), reconciliation may not always be possible. Nevertheless, when it *is* possible, the process of bringing that peace begins in us. For our final *Love Yourself* activity, you are invited to start this process, with the help of the Holy Spirit.

First, find a bridge. This can be a small secluded bridge in a park or a larger public bridge in your town; you may want to pick the size of the bridge based on the size of the conflict. Either way, once you've identified your bridge, go to it and walk out to the middle. While there, consider the ways that being a peacemaker is like building a bridge. A chasm has been created between you and someone else because of sin and brokenness. Making peace is like constructing a bridge over that conflict.

Close by praying these two prayers Louie offers in the session. Consider how they relate to the relationship you want to be reconciled:

> *God, I want you to be glorified in this more than I want to be right or wrong.*

> *God, I want this relationship restored, but you are going to have to do this in me.*

Stay as long as you need to, and consider journaling later about the experience in the space below.

You can trust God to lead you and empower you through this! As Paul reminds us in Philippians 1:6, "He who began a good work in you will carry it on to completion until the day of Christ Jesus." God started this in you, and God will finish it.

Trust him.

Pray. God is near.

The handshake of peace might not happen. But the Holy Spirit, through the power of the peace deal that God brokered with you, can give you the freedom to release others from all their wrongs—just like your heavenly Father released you from all of yours. And while you can't always reconcile, you can make a peace treaty with yourself, and you can, by the power of God at work in you, be free. You can retire from retaliation; you can bankrupt your endeavor of getting even; and you can walk with all the weight off of your shoulders. Because as far as it depended on you, you chose to live at peace with them.

Louie Giglio, Relat(able)

Love Your Neighbor: Watch Batman!

In 2005, director Christopher Nolan reinvented Batman for the silver screen with his bare-knuckle, grounded-in-reality take on the caped crusader. That film, *Batman Begins*, launched the "Dark Knight" trilogy and became the benchmark for all "serious" superhero movies to follow.

Your assignment for this final *Love Neighbor* exercise is to watch *Batman Begins* (perhaps with other people from this study) and reflect on its themes in light of this week's teaching on Romans 12. *Batman Begins* is a powerful presentation on the power of fear, as well as the distinction (or lack thereof) between justice and revenge.

After you watch the film, reflect on the following:

- Is there a difference between justice and revenge? Explain.

- What is the difference in the way Bruce answers this question as opposed to Ra's al Ghul?
- Is the way Batman uses fear a redemptive repurposing of it, or does it just cause more of the same problems?
- Do you think Bruce's Batman project is an example of "overcoming evil with good" or not?

bonus (session 1)

WHY DATE?

Is there a flame burning in your heart so that when you get to that moment—and Lord willing, you will—and you're standing at that altar, and your heart is in love with Jesus, is this other heart going to be just as in love with Jesus as yours?

Louie Giglio

Orientation

As mentioned in the Introduction, there are two "bonus" sessions included on the video for *Relat(able)* that you may decide to work through with your group members, or individually. This first bonus session is intended especially for those who are in dating relationships—or who can see themselves as being in a dating relationship in the future. In this session, Louie will stress that as we move closer in our love for *Jesus*, and the other person we're in the relationship with also moves closer in their love for *Jesus*, it ends up moving *both* of us closer to Jesus—and to each other. In the end, dating (and marriage) is not about the mate but about the Maker.

Welcome and Checking In

Go around the group and invite everyone to answer the following question:

What is a deal breaker for you in a dating relationship?

Hearing the Word

Read 2 Corinthians 6:14–16 aloud in the group. Invite everyone to listen for a fresh insight during the reading.

> [14] *Do not be yoked together with unbelievers. For what do righteousness and wickedness have in common? Or what fellowship can light have with darkness?* [15] *What harmony*

> *is there between Christ and Belial? Or what does a believer have in common with an unbeliever?* [16] *What agreement is there between the temple of God and idols? For we are the temple of the living God.*

Turn to the person next to you and take turns sharing your answers to the following questions:

What does the image of being "yoked" to someone else bring to mind? What is necessary for success?

What kinds of relationships are being described as "yoked" in these verses? What relationships with unbelievers does Paul encourage?

Why is dating an unbeliever a deal breaker? What is the purpose of an equally yoked marriage?

Watch the Video

Play the video segment for Bonus Session 1. As you watch, use the following outline to record any thoughts or concepts that stand out to you.

Notes

Dating has to be more than about *who* you date—you need to ask *why* you should be dating in the first place. You were created to bring glory to God, and the person you date should share this common purpose with you.

Marriage—and therefore dating—is not about the mate but about the mission.

Your mission to glorify God is going to inform your options right now. The person you date needs to have a heart just as in love with Jesus as yours is.

If the person you're dating doesn't know Jesus, then you're dating the wrong person. It won't work if you date a person who doesn't already have a heart beating for the common mission that's beating in your heart.

If you are not dating, the moment you are currently in is the most precious moment you have in relation to your future marriage. You can decide right now if you're the kind of person you would want to date. You can decide if you are ready for the person God wants to bring into your life or if there are areas you need to work on before that occurs.

You need to adjust to your "kingdom best" starting right now. If there is anything that has crept into your current relationship that is not kingdom best, you need to take whatever steps necessary to adjust right now.

Group Discussion

Take a few minutes with your group members to discuss what you just watched and explore these concepts in Scripture.

First Impressions

1. Before everyone shares in the large group, turn to one or two people next to you and finish this sentence: "After watching the video, one question I now have is . . ."

Community Reflection

2. What questions have you asked yourself in the past when thinking about dating someone?

3. How would you describe your relationship with Jesus? What makes that relationship grow? What pulls it apart?

4. Consider the person you are dating or the friends who are closest to you. According to 2 Corinthians 6:14–16, who would be considered "off limits" as a mate?

5. What kind of person do *you* want to be for your mate? What do you need to work on right now to start becoming that person?

6. What changes do you need to make in your current relationships to be prepared for God's kingdom best? What will making these changes cost you? What are the long-term benefits of making these changes now?

Becoming Relat(able)

For this activity, you will need an index card and pen or pencil for every person in the group. Note that there are two options for this exercise based on whether or not you are currently in a dating relationship.

If you are dating or feel you are ready to date: The pool of people with whom you are closest could likely hold the person you will date and eventually marry. For this reason, choosing these people wisely will have a long-term impact on your future marriage relationship. Write down three qualities that you are looking for in a mate, and then answer the following questions:

- Do you have any of these qualities? If so, which ones?
- If not, what can you do to develop these qualities in your life?

Now think about the people in your circle of friends—those who are the closest to you and know you the best. Do these friends possess these qualities, or do you need to surround yourself with a different set of people who love and honor Jesus more? If so, what steps will you take to begin to find those people?

If you aren't dating or ready to date: Write on an index card a specific area of your life where you need to grow more like Jesus (and keep it as a reminder). How can Jesus help you do this? Who has God put in your life to support you in becoming a person called to the mission of showing Jesus to the world? How could growing in this area prepare you for a God-honoring marriage?

Closing Prayer

End the meeting by inviting everyone in the group to pray silently for the person who may eventually become their mate. Ask God to prepare both of you to be faithful to his mission for you both and for his timing to bring you together.

bonus (session 2)

MARRIAGE WITH A MISSION

Submit to one another—not because you should, or ought to, or have to, or because it's a good idea that makes marriage better—but do it out of your reverence for Christ.

Louie Giglio

Orientation

This is the second bonus session included on the video for *Relat(able)*. Once again, based on the needs and composition of your group, you may decide to work through this material as an extension of your small group experience. This session is intended not only for married couples but also those who are engaged or even considering marriage at some future time. In this session, Louie will focus on the fact that there is more to marriage than just two people falling in love, for God has a mission for each of us who enter into this commitment. In the end, we will see that marriage is the *most sacred of all things* because it is a reflection of God's love and commitment to his people, called his church, through Christ.

Welcome and Checking In

Go around the group and invite everyone to answer the following questions:

> What are some famous marriages from history, film, literature, or television?
>
> What stands out to you about these marriages?

Hearing the Word

Read Ephesians 5:21 – 33 aloud in the group. Invite everyone to listen for a fresh insight during the reading.

21 Submit to one another out of reverence for Christ.

*22 Wives, submit yourselves to your own husbands as you
do to the Lord. 23 For the husband is the head of the wife as
Christ is the head of the church, his body, of which he is the
Savior. 24 Now as the church submits to Christ, so also wives
should submit to their husbands in everything.*

*25 Husbands, love your wives, just as Christ loved the
church and gave himself up for her 26 to make her holy, cleans-
ing her by the washing with water through the word, 27 and to
present her to himself as a radiant church, without stain or
wrinkle or any other blemish, but holy and blameless. 28 In this
same way, husbands ought to love their wives as their own bod-
ies. He who loves his wife loves himself. 29 After all, no one ever
hated their own body, but they feed and care for their body, just
as Christ does the church— 30 for we are members of his body.
31 "For this reason a man will leave his father and mother and
be united to his wife, and the two will become one flesh." 32 This
is a profound mystery—but I am talking about Christ and the
church. 33 However, each one of you also must love his wife as he
loves himself, and the wife must respect her husband.*

Turn to the person next to you and take turns sharing your answers to the following questions:

> What is the connection between submitting to each other and our relationship with Jesus?

How does Paul depict marriage? How does this picture influence the meaning of a husband and wife submitting to each other? How would you summarize the roles of the husband and wife presented in this passage?

How is Jesus, through his love for the church, a role model for husbands? How should this role benefit wives?

Watch the Video

Play the video segment for Bonus Session 2. As you watch, use the following outline to record any thoughts or concepts that stand out to you.

Notes

Marriage is not a ceremony, a party, or an exchanging of vows and rings. Marriage is a covenant, which is a binding agreement.

Your spouse is the most important relationship in your life on earth apart from Jesus. You have to prioritize that relationship and "align your orbits," because the relationship will become fragmented if you're not moving together in the same space.

When you talk to your spouse, allow for vulnerability without immediate retaliation. Have conversations that help you find out how your spouse is really doing—listen so your spouse feels safe in sharing and knows you won't make judgments or give criticism.

Show your spouse that your marriage is worth contending for. Everything on this planet is against your marriage, so you need to make choices that put your marriage before yourself.

Publicly and privately champion your spouse. Go on record publicly as being supportive of your spouse's efforts. Privately praise and encourage your spouse to show that you aren't just looking for attention but are sincerely applauding him or her.

Resign from the mission of changing your spouse, and adopt the greater mission of making God first in everything. Everything funnels into the mission, which comes out of the statement that "Jesus is everything."

Group Discussion

Take a few minutes with your group members to discuss what you just watched and explore these concepts in Scripture.

First Impressions

1. Before everyone shares in the large group, turn to one or two people next to you and finish this sentence: "After watching the video, one question I now have is …"

Community Reflection

2. How has your concept of marriage been different from the one presented in Scripture?

3. What can couples do to put Christ first in their lives? What impact would/does this have in your marriage?

4. Why is submission a difficult concept for most people? How is God's concept of submission different from the world's concept?

5. How can you build up and encourage your spouse? How do you think he or she would respond to your efforts?

6. How have you seen God use your marriage as an example to others of Jesus' love and sacrifice for the church? How can you strengthen this picture of God's love in your marriage?

Becoming Relat(able)

For this activity, you will need paper and pens or pencils for every couple in the group.

For the next few minutes, you will be spending some time writing a "mission statement" for your relationship. If you are married, this will be a mission statement for both you and your spouse. If you are dating or want to married, this will be a mission statement for what you want that future relationship to represent. As you write this statement, keep in mind the principles you learned during the video session.

Begin by stating the role God plays in your own life, and then indicate the role he plays in the other person's life (again, whether that is a spouse or boyfriend/girlfriend). Next, list three to five ways that you as a couple (or as a future couple) intend to fulfill your mission to "know Christ and make him known."

Allow several minutes to fine-tune what you have written. In the end, you want the mission statement to reflect your personalities as a couple (or future couple) and what God desires from you as a picture of his love for the church. Once you have a final draft, share what you have written with your group members, if you feel comfortable in doing so.

Finally, if you are married or in a dating relationship, set aside a time to formally commit to signing your mission statement as a couple. If you are not yet married or dating, commit to signing it as your intention to have a future marriage that honors God and serves to attract others into his kingdom. Put the mission statement in a place where you will see it frequently to serve as a reminder of your commitment.

Closing Prayer

End the meeting by asking God to give each couple a clear vision of his mission for their marriage. Pray that each marriage will grow in its likeness to Christ and that the ungodly influences of the world will be powerless to distort their mission.

ADDITIONAL RESOURCES FOR GROUP LEADERS

If you are reading this, then you have probably agreed to lead a *Relat(able)* group study. Thank you! What you have chosen to do is important, and much good fruit can come from studies like this. Thanks again for sharing your time and talent.

The *Relat(able)* experience is a six-session study built around video content and small group interaction. That's where you come in. As the group leader, imagine yourself as the host of a dinner party. Your job is to take care of your guests by managing all the behind-the-scenes details so that when everyone finally arrives, they can just enjoy one another.

As the group leader, your role is not to answer all the questions or reteach the content—the video and study guide will do most of that work. Your job is to guide the experience and cultivate your small group into a kind of teaching community. This will make it a place to process, question, and reflect—not receive more instruction.

As such, make sure everyone in the group gets a copy of the study guide. Encourage them to write in their guide and bring it with them every week. This will keep everyone on the same page and help the process run more smoothly.

As noted at the beginning of the study guide, this curriculum also features two bonus sessions, should you want to customize the experience for groups of married couples and those planning or considering marriage ("Marriage with a Mission") or those who are dating or thinking about dating ("Why Date?"). These bonus sessions include video segments but no personal study sections.

Hospitality

As group leader you'll want to create an environment conducive to sharing and learning. A church sanctuary or formal classroom may not be ideal for this kind of meeting because those venues can feel formal and less intimate. Wherever you choose, make sure there is enough comfortable seating for everyone and, if possible, arrange the seats in a semicircle so everyone can see the video easily. This will make the transition between the video and group conversation more efficient and natural.

Also, try to get to the meeting site early so you can greet participants as they arrive, especially newcomers. Simple refreshments create a welcoming atmosphere and can be a wonderful addition to a group study gathering. If you do serve food, try to take into account any food allergies or dietary restrictions your group may have. Also, if you meet in a home, you will want to find out if the house has pets (in case there are any allergies), and even consider offering child care to couples with children who want to attend.

Finally, be sure your media technology is working properly. Managing these details up front will make the rest of your group experience flow effectively and provide a welcoming space in which to engage the content of *Relat(able)*.

Leading Your Group

Once everyone has arrived, it will be time to begin the group. If you are new to leading small groups, what follows are some simple tips to make your group time healthy, enjoyable, and effective.

First, consider beginning the meeting with a word of prayer. Then remind people to silence and put away their mobile phones. This is a way to say yes to being present to each other and to God.

Next, invite someone to read the session's "Orientation" from the study guide. This will get everyone on the same page regarding that week's content. Then, after the "Welcome and Checking In" time (see below), your group will engage in a simple Bible study drawn from video content called "Hearing the Word." You do not need to be a biblical scholar to lead this effectively. Your role is only to open up conversation by using the instructions provided and to invite the group into the text.

Now that the group is fully engaged, it is time to watch the video. The content of each *Relat(able)* session is inspiring and challenging, so there is built-in time for personal reflection before anyone is asked to respond. Don't skip over this part. Internal processors will need more intimate space to sort through their thoughts and questions, and it will make the group discussion time more fruitful.

During the group discussion, encourage everyone in the group to participate, but make sure that those who do not want to share (especially as the questions become more personal) know they do not have to do so. As the discussion progresses, follow up with questions like, "Tell me more about that," or "Why did you answer the way you did?" This will allow participants to deepen their reflections, and it invites meaningful sharing in a nonthreatening way.

You have been given multiple questions to use in each session. You do not have to use them all or follow them in order. Feel free to pick and choose questions based on either the needs of your group or how the conversation is flowing. Also, don't be afraid of silence. Offering a question and allowing up to thirty seconds of silence gives people space to think about how they want to respond and also gives them time to do so.

As group leader, you are the boundary keeper for your group. Do not let anyone (yourself included) dominate the discussion. Keep an eye out for group members who might be tempted to "attack" folks they disagree with or try to "fix" those having struggles. Such behaviors can derail a group's momentum, so you need to discourage them from taking place. Model active listening and encourage everyone in your group to do the same. This will make your group time a safe space and foster the kind of community that God can use to change people.

The group discussion time leads to the final and most dynamic part of this study, "Becoming Relat(able)." During this section participants are invited to transform what they have learned into practical action. However, for this to be successful will require some preparation on your part. Take time to read over each session's "Becoming Relat(able)" segment, as several of them require special materials. Reading ahead will allow you to ask group members to bring any items you might need but don't have, and it will give you a sense of how to lead your group through these experiences. Use the supply list below to make sure you have what you need for each session.

Supply List

Session 1

- Pens (one for each group member)
- Blank pieces of paper (one for each group member)
- Envelopes (one for each group member)
- (Optional) Paper clips for attaching the envelope to the study guide

Session 2

- Current newspapers, news magazines, or smartphones with web browsers

Session 5

- 8½ x 11 sheets of paper (one for each group member)

Session 6

- Small bucket three-fourths full of water
- Small stones (at least one per participant). (These stones can be found outside, or you can get decorative ones at a craft or hardware store.)

Bonus Session 1

- Index cards (one for each group member)
- Pens or pencils (one for each group member)

Bonus Session 2

- Paper and pens or pencils for every couple in the group

Finally, even though instructions are provided for how to conclude each session, please feel free to strike out on your own. Just make sure you do something intentional to mark the end of the meeting. It may also be helpful to take time before or after the closing prayer to go over that week's *Love God, Love Yourself,* and *Love Your Neighbor* options. This will allow people to consider what they would like to try or ask any questions they have so everyone can depart in confidence.

Debriefing the Between Session Materials

As just noted, each session includes an on-your-own section where everyone is invited to choose one or more of these activities: *Love God, Love Yourself,* or *Love Your Neighbor*. Your job at the beginning of the current week's session is to help the group members debrief the previous week's experience. This time is called "Welcome and Checking In."

Debriefing something like this is a bit different from responding to questions based on the video because the content comes from the participants' real lives. Though you are free to direct this time as you prefer, the basic experiences that you want the group to reflect on are:

- What was the best thing about the activity?
- What was the hardest thing about it?
- What did you learn about yourself?
- What did you learn about God?

There are specific debriefing questions to help process each activity; however, the aforementioned areas are what the "Checking In" time is designed to explore.